AMAZING FAMILY ADVENTURES

by Jen and Sim Benson

First published in the United Kingdom in 2017
by National Trust Books
43 Great Ormond Street
London WC1N 3HZ

An imprint of Pavilion Books Group

ISBN: 9781909881877

A CIP catalogue record for this book is available from the British Library.

10 9 8 7 6 5 4 3 2 1

Reproduction by Colourdepth, UK
Printed by Times Offset (Malaysia) Sdn Bhd

This book can be ordered direct from the publisher at the website: www.pavilionbooks.com, or try your local bookshop.

Also available at
National Trust shops or
www.shop.nationaltrust.org.uk

Contents

SECTION 1.

Starting out: Easy adventures for everyone

1. Follow a waymarked trail 18
2. Explore a rock pool 22
3. Go foraging 26
4. Go on a night walk 30
5. Wildlife safari: parks and gardens 34
6. Wildlife safari: woodland and forest 40
7. Wildlife safari: lakes and ponds 46
8. Hunt for fossils 52
9. A winter beach adventure 56
10. Celebrate a festival 60
11. Take a boat trip 64
12. A barefoot adventure 68
13. Circumnavigate a lake 72
14. A wild weather adventure 76
15. Watch the sunrise 80
16. A literary adventure 84
17. Go glamping! 88

SECTION 2.

The next step: Bigger challenges for up and coming adventurers

18. Explore a castle 94
19. Help out on the farm 98
20. Make a raft and sail it 102
21. Complete a Parkrun 106
22. Explore a cave 108
23. Make a home for a creature 112
24. Create an adventure journal 114
25. Go tree climbing 116
26. Explore a film set 120
27. Go sledging 124
28. Fly a kite 128
29. Walk in a stream 132
30. Climb to the top of a tower 136
31. Travel back in time 138
32. Be a volunteer 142
33. Go on a bat walk 146
34. Go camping 150

SECTION 3.

A step further: Great adventures in wild places

35. An island adventure 156
36. Track a wild animal 160
37. Climb a mountain 164
38. Wilderness survival and bushcraft 168
39. Go bouldering 172
40. Camp in the wild 176
41. Paddle your own canoe 180
42. Ride a mountain bike trail 184
43. Explore a waterfall 188
44. Go wild swimming 192
45. Go orienteering 196
46. Sleep in a bothy 200

SECTION 4.

Giant leaps: Extreme challenges for the brave and bold

47. Go ghyll scrambling and coasteering 206
48. A sea kayaking adventure 210
49. Rock climbing and abseiling 214
50. Surf's up! 218

INTRODUCTION

Being outdoors is great for families. Wide open spaces to run around in, gardens and parks to explore, woodland trails to follow with trees to climb and dens to build along the way, rivers to dam, sand to dig and waves to jump. The abundance of play – for all ages – to be found, effortlessly, in the natural world is something to be wholeheartedly embraced and celebrated.

The National Trust's Natural Childhood report highlights the hugely positive influence that regular contact with nature has on children, alongside the increasing difficulty in providing this. A 2015 survey by the Wildlife Trusts found that over 90% of people agree that our wellbeing and quality of life is based on nature and biodiversity. Yet biodiversity continues to decline and evidence suggests we are becoming increasingly detached from our natural world.

We believe that families – parents, grandparents, guardians, siblings, extended families – are the key to ensuring every child has the opportunity to develop a personal connection with the natural world, with all the benefits this brings. Family adventures – times when fun is had, experiences shared and challenges overcome as a family – bring people and nature together, and create memories and bonds that last a lifetime.

Hand-in-hand with the need to connect with nature is the need to protect it. The National Trust takes its conservation duties seriously, looking after over 600,000 acres of land of outstanding

Left: A woodland walk in the Surrey Hills.
Above left: Family trip along the river.

Above right: Pond dipping at Clumber Park, Nottinghamshire.

natural beauty and over 775 miles (1,200km) of coastline. This work helps to ensure that the natural environment that is so important to us, as human beings, is preserved for the benefit and enjoyment of future generations.

Mountains and moorland, forests and rivers provide an incredible arena for learning and play, but it's not just wild places that are fantastic for family adventures. There are castles to invade, spooky houses to explore and fascinating stories of days gone by to be discovered. This is no ordinary history lesson: it's a 3D, interactive, multi-sensory experience that will be talked about for years to come.

We've often said that stepping into a National Trust place is a form of relaxation in its own right. Perhaps it's the gently child-friendly way they're managed; or the abundance of smiling volunteers who seem to have endless time for our daughter's questions; or the legacy of history's greatest architects and landscapers exerting their influence from centuries past. Whatever the reasons, wherever we go it seems to work brilliantly: a warm café; a cold ice-cream; a perfectly placed bench or a view to admire. These places are timeless and – we hope – will have something that appeals to every family member, regardless of their age or ability. It's hard to please the whole family the whole of the time, but we love a challenge and our guiding principle is to find and include an adventure for everyone.

How to use this book

This book is organised by adventure and divided into sections that ascend in their level of challenge. As a rough guide, the adventures included are suitable for:

SECTION 1
STARTING OUT:
Easy adventures for everyone (ages 0–4).

SECTION 2
THE NEXT STEP:
Bigger challenges for up-and-coming adventurers (ages 5–7).

SECTION 3
A STEP FURTHER:
Great adventures in wild places (ages 8–11).

SECTION 4
GIANT LEAPS:
Extreme challenges for the brave and bold (older children).

We recognise, however, that abilities vary greatly and even those who are capable of some of the extreme activities such as gorge scrambling or rock climbing might equally enjoy a stroll around the woods or a paddle in the sea. The divisions are therefore mainly based on their level of challenge, so you can pick and choose depending on what you fancy doing, how much time and effort you want to expend doing it and what you feel you are capable of undertaking safely.

Key to symbols

- Café
- Buggy/baby-friendly
- Play area
- Dog-friendly
- Toilets
- Hazards – take care
- Learning
- Wildlife
- Beach
- Campsite
- Restaurant
- Pub
- Shop
- Cycling
- 50 Things to do before you're 11¾ (see page 7)

A practical guide to family adventuring

Planning

When it comes to planning adventures, kids love to be involved. Get the map out and all have a look at an area and its potential for exploration. Younger children love identifying key features such as forests, rivers and roads, while older children may be able to start relating the contours to the landscape – it's a great way to start becoming familiar with the art of navigation. Ask the children for their suggestions and make sure your day out includes something for everyone. Fill everyone in on the basics, including what time you need to leave the house and what everyone needs to bring with them. Organise your kit, food and water and have it all ready to go the night before, especially if you're starting out early. The better your planning, the smoother the day will run.

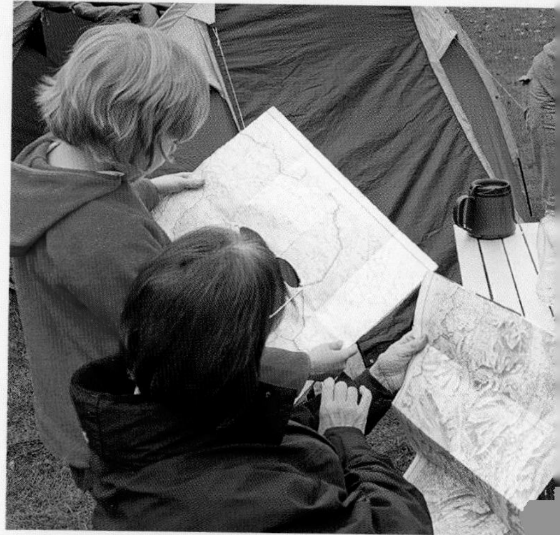

Planning at Great Langdale campsite, Cumbria.

Get inspired!

There are many sources of inspiration when it comes to family adventuring. Think about places near home to start with: is there a hill you've always wanted to climb or a bridge that would be perfect for pooh-sticks? Find out where other families enjoy exploring – local internet forums are great for this – but don't be afraid to make up your own adventures either. Use the seasons to guide you too: forage blackberries in autumn, look for snowdrops at the beginning of the year or bluebells later in spring. The National Trust Handbook and website are great sources of information – or kids can join the 50 things website (www.nationaltrust.org.uk/50-things-to-do) for fun ideas and activity tick lists.

Clothing and footwear

It's amazing how much clothing younger children can need over the course of a

day. Pack changes of clothes for when they get wet and muddy, warm layers, waterproofs and plenty of spare socks! Kids get warm running around but cool down rapidly once they stop, so layering is a good idea and allows for easy temperature regulation. Make sure footwear fits correctly, is light in weight, lets the foot move naturally and has a good sole. Children are literally finding their feet when they go adventuring, so it's important that they can trust their footwear and aren't hampered by shoes that will be uncomfortable if they're too small, trip them up if they're too big, or discourage them from exploring if they don't have good grip.

It's also important to think about clothing choices for adults and older kids when you're heading into remote and/ or exposed areas. In cold, dry weather lightweight insulation such as down or Primaloft jackets are a great choice; they can be stashed away in a rucksack when you're working hard walking up a hill but provide invaluable warmth on the way back down. A lightweight waterproof is also a great item to take with you – it's versatile and can be worn over a light baselayer in warmer weather or as part of a layering system in cold, wet, windy weather. Again, your choice of footwear will have a big impact on your enjoyment. Well-fitting, water-resistant walking boots or shoes with a sole that you trust will make the day safer and much more fun – especially if you end up on carrying duty.

Jumping the waves at Brancaster Beach, Norfolk.

Equipment

Adventures with really young children can be a great way for new parents to spend some quality time together and get back into the great outdoors. A good off-road buggy with suspension, rugged tyres and brakes can make a walk in the woods an enjoyable excursion, and the good ones will handle rough terrain with ease. Many National Trust places have off-road buggies you can borrow for the day for free. Our own adventures take us up mountains and over stiles, so we opted for baby carriers when our kids were little. Soft rucksack-style carriers such as the Ergobaby, Mountain Buggy Juno and Boba carriers are a great choice for getting out and about on more rugged terrain with babies and smaller children. These can be worn on the front, back or side and keep the child close so you can monitor – and share – body heat. They also enable you to carry your child's weight close to your centre of mass, which is efficient and safer over rough terrain. Soft carriers and slings pack small enough to fit easily into a rucksack and, if you're up for carrying them, will transport a child

On the beach at Alnmouth, Northumberland.

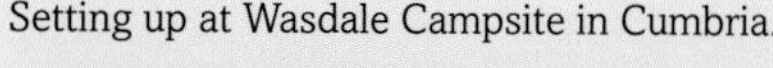

Setting up at Wasdale Campsite in Cumbria.

up to around the age of 4, so they're a great item to take along on a walk in case a child wants carrying any distance. You can also get warm and/or waterproof covers that provide an excellent level of protection for the child.

A good, well-fitting rucksack is essential for carrying all the things that will make any adventure much more fun for everyone. Make sure it has plenty of external pockets to allow for easy access to water, snacks, wet wipes and so on – it's frustrating to have to keep stopping and rummaging around in the main compartment otherwise. A waterproof cover is a good addition, and we insert a drybag into the bag if it's a wet day so that anything inside is doubly protected – particularly important if you're carrying things like cameras, nappies and dry clothing. Kids often like to carry a few of their own items in a small rucksack, allowing them to feel a useful part of the whole experience.

It's essential to carry a few emergency items if you're anywhere remote or weather-affected. Pack a basic first aid kit, torch, map, compass, whistle and mobile phone. For mountain excursions we'll also pack an emergency shelter – a packable waterproof cover that's big enough for us all to fit under – which is bright enough to be spotted from a distance and would keep us all warm and dry if needed. It can seem a bit extreme to pack this kind of thing for a straightforward walk up a

Enjoying a cream tea at Parke, Devon.

mountain, but it means you're equipped to deal with any eventualities that you meet along the way.

Camping and other specialist activities such as climbing and mountain-biking require a full list of items in their own right; these are discussed in more detail later in the book.

Food and drink

One of the many great things about adventuring on National Trust property is the availability of fantastic cafés and restaurants serving excellent food and drink that, wherever possible, is sourced and crafted locally. From estate-reared venison to locally made ice-cream there's always something to suit every palate. As sleep-deprived parents ourselves we're happy to report that the coffee's good too! Finishing a walk or bike ride at a café can be a great way to motivate the whole family, and food tastes so much better when it's enjoyed after a hard day's adventuring.

When you're venturing into wilder places it's important to pack plenty of food and water for the whole family. Kids require regular refuelling when they're exercising, particularly in colder weather, so keep a supply readily available. Keep an eye out for the usual signs – going quiet, whining or stopping – and step in with a well-timed snack.

Walking the Bath Skyline, Somerset.

Finding your way

Learning to read a map is a great skill for everyone: it's enjoyable, empowering and incredibly useful – and you don't have to rely on batteries or mobile/GPS signals either. There are some brilliant ways to get started in navigating, while having fun as a family too. Try:

- following arrows on a waymarked walk
- using a simplified map to find your way around a park
- geocaching – set up a free account at geocaching.com and use a GPS device to find 'caches'
- orienteering using a map and compass on a pre-set course
- enrolling on a navigation course and heading out into the wilds to test out your skills

Many National Trust places have one or more of these activities available for you to try out – check online, contact your local places or read on for suggestions.

Get involved

Adventuring with kids can be challenging but it can also be incredibly rewarding. Being with your children while they discover something for the first time, whether it's dipping a baby's toes in a stream, paddling with a toddler, or swimming in the sea with older kids, is an experience to treasure. Try climbing a tree, helping with den building or rediscovering the cartwheel: it's wonderfully liberating and your kids will love seeing you joining in. They might even be impressed at your skills!

Den building at Kingston Lacy, Dorset.

Learn as you go

Adventuring is a great way for the whole family to learn new things. Kids are naturally questioning – we're amazed how much we learn just by looking up the answers to their questions. Try naming things you see as you go. If you don't know the name of something, take a photo or commit it to memory and look it up later. There are some great apps available for nature identification, and kids of all ages enjoy getting involved in using these. We've also included some spotting sheets with this book to get you started.

Tying adventures in with a topic that children are covering at school, or have a particular interest in, is a great way to stimulate learning in a multi-dimensional way. Visiting a castle or a Roman site; taking a really close look at some rocks; even using pebbles to practise basic

maths are all great ways to incorporate a bit of learning. Using the day's experiences to create a poster, picture or poem reinforces knowledge and deepens understanding.

Share the experience

Sharing adventures with others creates strong friendships, brings a greater variety of skills to the trip and can be a huge amount of fun. Meet up with another family; take the in-laws along or ask older children to invite a friend. Group adventures that involve camping work particularly well with others as there are more people to share kit-carrying and tent-pitching duties, and more campfire stories to be told.

Make it fun

Having a rewarding and enjoyable adventure will leave everyone wanting to do it again. Be prepared to put in some work and overcome some challenges in order to make the trip a success, but don't be afraid to turn around or change your goal if that feels like the best decision. If you're intending to climb to the top of a hill but in practice simply have a great time skimming stones and paddling in the stream at the bottom, consider it a successful adventure. The aim is to get outside somewhere beautiful together, expend some energy and have fun.

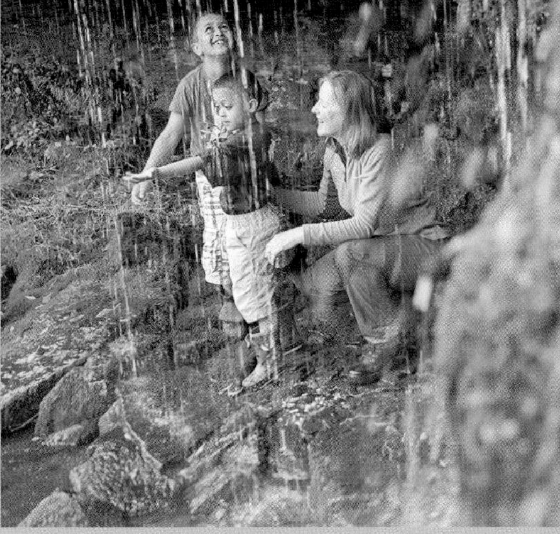

Playing behind Crook Gill waterfall, Yorkshire.

A brief note on safety

Family adventures that happen within the grounds of an estate are relatively safe and require minimal planning. However venturing into wilder, more remote and weather-affected areas carries the potential for getting lost, injured or cold. Plan well, take emergency equipment, tell someone where you're going and what time you expect to be back and make sure you know what to do if things don't go to plan.

The National Trust make every effort to inform their visitors of obvious dangers, but the natural environment does carry inherent risks that they are unable to manage. Prior to undertaking any outdoor activity please do ensure that you are confident that such activities can be undertaken safely, having regard to the environmental conditions and your own fitness and technical ability.

Best for

Home is where you pitch it.

Best for beaches

- Brancaster, Norfolk
- Ravenscar, North Yorkshire
- Barafundle Bay, Pembrokeshire
- Compton Bay, Isle of Wight
- Formby, Liverpool
- Studland, Dorset

Best for picnics

- Rowallane Garden, County Down
- The Weir Garden, Herefordshire
- Dunham Massey, Cheshire
- Wallington, Northumberland

Best for buggies

- Stowe, Buckinghamshire
- Killerton, Devon
- Cragside, Northumberland
- Tarn Hows, Cumbria
- Gibside, Tyne and Wear
- Penrhyn Castle, Gwynedd

Best for teenagers

- Belton House, Lincolnshire
- Great Langdale, Cumbria
- Strangford Lough, County Down
- Stackpole, Pembrokeshire
- Lacock Abbey, Wiltshire
- Croyde, Devon

Best for wildlife

- Brownsea Island, Dorset
- Wicken Fen and Hoe Fen, Cambridgeshire
- Dunwich Heath, Suffolk
- Farne Islands, Northumberland
- Lyme Park, Cheshire
- Llŷn Peninsula, Snowdonia

Best for events/festivals

- Dyrham Park, Gloucestershire
- Stackpole, Pembrokeshire
- Downhill Demesne, County Londonderry
- Killerton, Devon
- Fountains Abbey, North Yorkshire
- Stowe, Buckinghamshire

Best for camping

- Lake District campsites, Cumbria
- Clumber Park, Nottinghamshire
- Castle Ward, County Down
- Highertown Farm, Cornwall
- Hafod y Llan, Snowdonia
- Polesden Lacey, Surrey

Best for sports

- Stourhead, Wiltshire
- Penrose, Cornwall
- Stackpole, Pembrokeshire
- Osterley Park, London
- Great Langdale, Cumbria
- Longshaw, Derbyshire

Ultimate family weekends

Weekend 1: Great Langdale, Cumbria

- Camp at the National Trust's Great Langdale campsite; wake up to fresh croissants for breakfast and views of rugged peaks
- Venture into the woods, climb trees, build dens and spot wildlife
- Make a raft and sail it on the little stream that runs through the campsite or walk up to Stickle Tarn and sail it on open water
- Paddle in the shallows of Stickle Tarn, or see how far you can skim a stone
- Go ghyll scrambling
- Climb Side Pike for views all the way back down to your tent
- Have a warming meal at the National Trust's Sticklebarn pub

Weekend 2: Brownsea Island, Dorset

- Catch the boat from Sandbanks across to the island
- Stay in one of only two holiday cottages on the island (both run by the National Trust), with views from the window straight out across the harbour
- Explore the island, watching out for red squirrels, peacocks, deer and little egrets
- Have ice-cream at the café, watching the boats go by
- Catch a ferry over to Studland and play on the white sandy beaches, fly a kite, swim in the sea or hire a kayak or stand-up-paddle board to explore the waves
- Watch the sun set from the secret island beach at Maryland

Ghyll scrambling in Stickle Ghyll, Great Langdale.

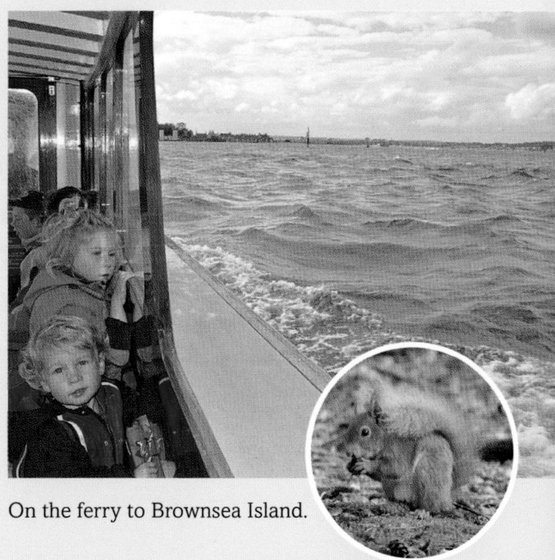

On the ferry to Brownsea Island.

EASY ADVENTURES FOR EVERYONE

A great place to start for families with younger children, this chapter is a gentle introduction to the world of adventuring. From a waymarked walk or a trip in a boat to spotting seals or simply watching the sun rise, these are all enjoyable ways to inspire a passion for the great outdoors and learn the skills required for a lifetime of adventures.

1 Follow a waymarked trail

Waymarked walks are a great way to introduce children to the art of finding their way around a landscape. With a range of distances there's always a route to suit everyone and no need to worry about getting lost. Children love spotting the different coloured arrows and having control over their adventure, with endless opportunities for exploration along the way. Simple route plans are available at many National Trust places, and these are a great introduction to map reading, with orienteering and geocaching being the next step up. Children also love a 'point' to a walk, rather than simply heading out for exercise or enjoyment.

One of our favourite walks winds through woodland at the Parke Estate on the edge of Dartmoor, Devon. Three exciting trails lead you on three different adventures, each one marked with its

GREAT FOR BUGGY-FRIENDLY · YOUNGER KIDS · NATURE · ACTIVE

own set of coloured arrows. Finding the next arrow provides a natural stimulus to keep moving (often a challenge in its own right with toddlers) and a simple, regular reward. Even the most straightforward route includes a boardwalk, a fast-flowing stream with a pebble beach and some steep climbs. The hardest of the trails is much longer – a proper day out – with tricky terrain and greater distances between arrows. It's a nice choice to have and a good way to gradually increase the level of challenge – and all three finish at the café for post-adventure ice-cream. There are often seasonal or themed events at National Trust places that include a trail to follow, from Easter egg hunts with chocolate at the end to puzzles that involve finding clues. Kids love to get involved and it makes a day out at a house or garden a more enjoyable, interactive experience for them.

Of course, following a series of clues is something you can do almost anywhere. Older children might like to set their own trails, or you could set one for younger kids as a way of exploring a local park, forest or even the garden. Using obvious signs, such as sticks arranged in an arrow shape to point the way; small piles of flour or sawdust; written clues to be found and decoded; or even a more subtle trail, can create an enjoyable treasure hunt, especially if there's a prize at the end.

Following a trail at Eskdale, Cumbria.

Following the arrows at Allan Bank, Cumbria.

FUN FACTS

- Many National Trust places have waymarked trails with walks of varying lengths to suit everyone.
- Children love spotting arrows and showing everyone else the way. Older kids might like to have a go at using the map to find their way too.

1

Follow a waymarked trail

Where to go

SOUTH WEST

Parke

near Bovey Tracey, Devon TQ13 9JQ

 (not National Trust)

Parke has three excellent, adventurous waymarked walks with arrows in different colours, perfect for younger children to spot. Many paths are buggy-friendly and there's an enclosed, dog-free area near the café where small children can play safely. This is an exciting location on the edge of Dartmoor with a river and pebbly beach and lots of wildlife to spot.

WEST MIDLANDS

Croft Castle

Yarpole, near Leominster, Herefordshire HR6 9PW

Croft Castle is a huge, beautiful castle with 'proper' turrets that will impress even the most demanding knight-to-be. There's even a mini version for children to play in. The estate is perfect for picnics and there's a wild play area and waymarked walks, some of which are specifically designed for children.

Walking in the grounds of Croft Castle, Herefordshire.

NORTH EAST

Wallington

Cambo, near Morpeth, Northumberland NE61 4AR

Explore secret gardens with ponds perfect for wildlife safaris. There's an adventure playground, a play train and a 'wild' woodland, perfect for tree-climbing. Or head out into the 13,000 acres of lush estate, packed with a variety of walks to suit all abilities.

Codger's Fort, on the estate at Wallington, Northumberland.

2 Explore a rock pool

We love exploring rock pools; waiting for the tide to recede, exposing gleaming windows into the underwater world. There's always so much to see, from blue-black oval mussels and pale crescent clams to spiny starfish and skittering crabs. It's a great winter activity, when it's too cold to venture more than a toe's depth into the sea. South Devon's Wembury is one of our favourite places to go, with its rugged coastline that dips to a beautiful section of beach. There's plenty of sand for digging and castling, but it's the rocky plateau that curves around the bay and extends out towards the wedge-shaped Mewstone that hides the real gems here.

One cold January day we set out, a small hand in each of ours, balancing carefully on the grippy, barnacle-encrusted rocks as we made our way away from the beach, following the receding tide. The first few pools we reached held a few treasures: dark red, slimy-looking beadlet anemones; limpets and the occasional crab. The further out towards the sea we ventured the more we found: blue-green snakelocks anemones whose tentacles wave in the gentle currents; common blennies – also known as sea-

FUN FACTS

- Rock pools are tidal pools that are usually submerged at high tide and exposed as the sea-level falls.
- There are many creatures and plants to be found in Britain's rock pools: look for anemones, shore crabs, pipe fish, sea scorpion, spiny star fish, sucker fish, edible crabs and limpets.

frogs as they can breathe above as well as below the water – that bury themselves deep within crevices or under rocks until disturbed; and even a constellation of tiny starfish, known as cushion stars, the smallest in the UK.

Rock-pooling is a great activity, in any size of group, at any time of the year. It's lovely to go as a family, spotting things, taking photos and looking anything you're not sure about up later. Or you can ask one of the local experts – such as those at the Wembury Marine Centre – for their opinion.

Rock-pooling at Birling Gap and the Seven Sisters, East Sussex.

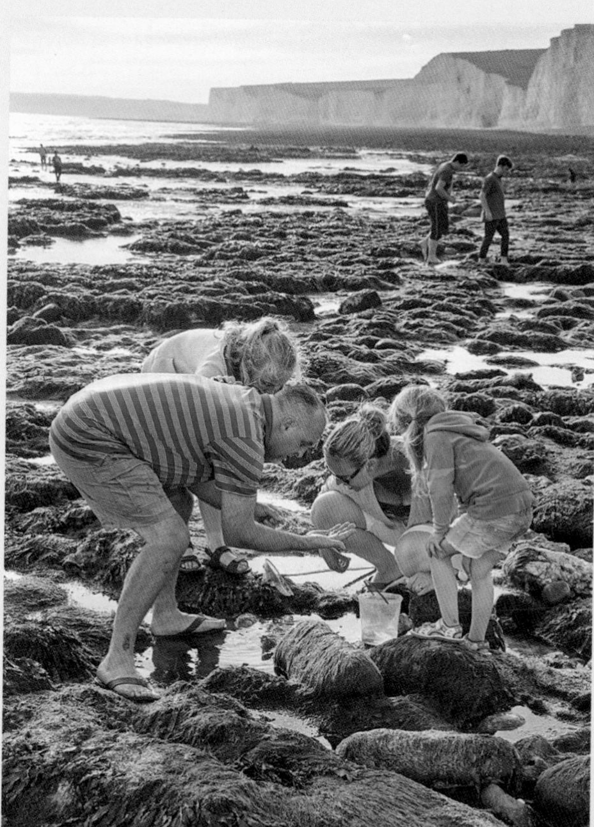

TOP TIPS

- The creatures that live in rock pools are delicate: be very careful if you handle them, don't accidentally tread on them, and return them all to their homes once you've had a look.
- Use your hands to remove anything from a rock pool; nets, buckets and spades can damage the delicate habitat.
- Only take empty shells (and your litter!) home with you.
- Keep an eye on the tide at all times so you don't get caught out.
- The best time to go rock-pooling is about an hour either side of low tide, giving you a good couple of hours' exploring time. A low spring tide will uncover the greatest number of pools.

GREAT FOR BIG ADVENTURES • NATURE • ACTIVE

Where to go

SOUTH

St Helens Duver

St Helens, Isle of Wight PO33 1XY

This is a great place for kids as there's everything you need for a family day out within easy reach: sandy beaches to play on; woodland to explore; dunes to run down; and rock pools to gaze into. It can get quite busy in summer, but head further along the coast and you'll probably have the beach all to yourself. There's wildlife galore; fascinating history with archaeological findings that date back to the Stone Age and holiday cottages nearby if you want to stay for longer.

NORTHERN IRELAND

Strangford Lough

Strangford, County Down

At 150km², Strangford Lough is the largest sea lough in the British Isles. It's a perfect place for budding naturalists, with over 2,000 species of marine wildlife to be found in or around the water. There's a great choice of places to stay nearby: sleep under the stars at one of the shore-side campsites, cosy up in a wool-insulated wooden pod or hire the Salt Island bothy, which sleeps up to eight people. You might spot one of five species of bat that live here, hear seals barking and otters playing or watch red squirrels jumping through the trees.

SOUTH WEST

Wembury Beach

Wembury, Devon PL9 0HP

Winter only (not National Trust)

In our opinion, Wembury is one of the very best places to go rock-pooling. Intriguing rock formations create fascinating bowls, trenches and basins where you'll find crabs, anemones, starfish and limpets. It's a popular surfing venue, so you can often watch surfers playing on the waves. The beach is dog-free from May to September and the café is National Trust-owned but not managed so check opening times. There are also some great walks from the beach along the spectacular South West Coast Path.

Playing with seaweed at Wembury Beach in Devon.

3 Go foraging

In our busy modern lives food is often picked, prepared and packaged for us before we even see it. It's easy to forget the connection between food and nature, and younger children may have very little grasp of this at all. Growing a few easy things in pots or in the garden is a great way to introduce them to the life-cycle of each plant and our food's need for water, sunshine and nourishment. It's rewarding for children to plant, nurture and harvest something of their very own too.

Foraging is a wonderful way to reconnect with our roots as gatherers and grazers; it's something many of us do naturally when we pass a hedge laden with late summer blackberries, or walk beneath a tree heavy with plump, purple damsons. But this is just the start! If you know where – and when – to look, there's a banquet of free, nutritious food that's readily available and an adventure to find. Remember: only pick where the plant grows in abundance and don't disturb or damage habitats. Many National Trust places offer guided foraging walks and courses – a great introduction to wild food and how to enjoy it safely and responsibly.

Whortleberries, hurts, blaeberries, whimberries or bilberries (depending on where in the country you find them) are one of our favourite things to forage. They're very rewarding, especially for small children, as they're abundant, easy to reach and prickle-free, taste great and require no preparation. Resembling small blueberries, they grow in some of Britain's most beautiful places, making for some

FUN FACTS

- Wild plants are protected by law in the UK but foliage, flowers and fruit are not, so these can be foraged, as long as you have permission to be on the property where they grow.
- Stinging nettles are one of the most widely available, easily identifiable and versatile wild plants. Their sting is deactivated with mild heat. Wear gloves to pick them, wash them well and use them like spring greens. Be inventive: soups, pestos, stir-fries and curries work brilliantly with nettles.
- Of the 10,000 different food plants known, 150 have been cultivated and just 20 provide 90% of the world's food requirements today.

Foraging for sweet chestnuts.

delightful days out – and a great snack on the go. We've picked them on the Welsh mountainsides in the Brecon Beacons and the Rhinogs; alongside the River Dart in Devon; and on Derbyshire's Peak District fells. They're delicious straight from the bush, but can also be made into jam or put in pies or crumbles. And it's not just hedgerows of course – coastal locations are abundant with wild food if you know where to look, from seafood to seaweed. June, July and August are the best months to pick samphire, a delicious plant that tastes a little like asparagus. You'll find it in saltmarsh and mudflats.

TOP TIPS

- If you're not sure, don't eat it. Stick to unmistakable varieties that you're 100% certain are safe.
- When cooking with foraged ingredients, start with a little and add more if you like it. Wild flavours can be much stronger than the cultivated ones we're used to.
- Keep your eyes peeled for foraging spots whenever you go walking: hedgerows are some of the best places to look, with treasures such as blackberries, raspberries, and hazelnuts to be found.

Children taking part in a 'crumble rumble' at Hughenden, Buckinghamshire.

GREAT FOR NATURE • ACTIVE • CREATIVE

Where to go

SOUTH WEST

Hembury and Holne Woods

Dartmoor, Devon

These lush, green ancient oak woodlands are a magical place for an adventure filled with wildlife and a great spot for foraging too. Mushrooms, whortleberries, nuts and blackberries are among the delights you'll find here. The River Dart flows through it all, perfect for paddling, swimming or skimming stones.

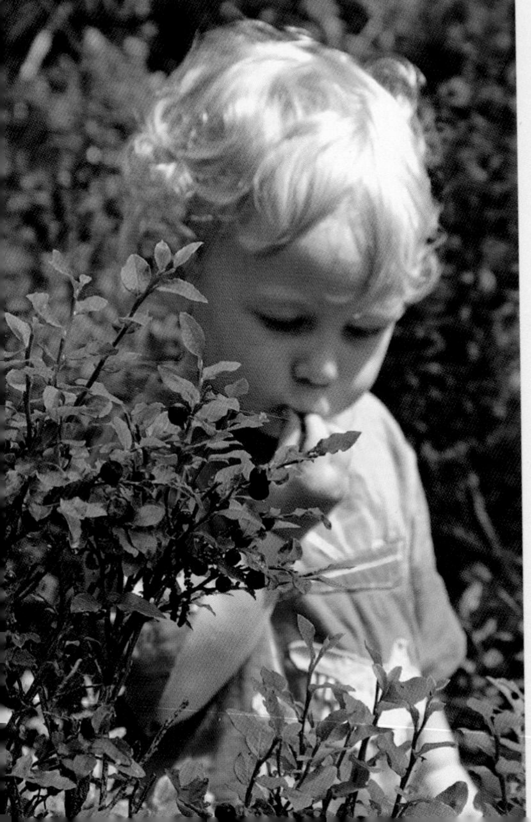

SOUTH WEST

Studland and Knoll Beach

near Swanage, Dorset BH19 3AH

(on leads)

From seafood to seaweed there's plenty of wild food for free on Britain's coastlines. Studland's rangers run a kayak foraging trip where you'll learn what you can eat and how to catch it. If you'd prefer there's delicious fish and chips available from the Knoll beach café, and plenty to keep everyone entertained on the beach from kite flying and sandcastling to sea swimming and boat hire.

Foraging wild whortleberries in Hembury Woods, Devon.

NORTH

Roseberry Topping

Newton-under-Roseberry, North Yorkshire TS9 6QR

(not National Trust)

Wild garlic is one of the easiest things to forage and it grows in abundance at Roseberry Topping. This popular landmark, Yorkshire's mini Matterhorn, is a thoroughly enjoyable – and achievable – climb to the sharp summit where glorious views await.

Roseberry Topping, North Yorkshire.

4 Go on a night walk

It's amazing how little time we spend in real darkness; with electric lighting through the winter and long, light evenings in summer it's easy to forget what a delight it is simply to be outside in the dark. A warm night, if you can, is best, when there will be the most to listen to in the night around you. As the last light grows dim, bats flick through the air catching insects, the last birdsong fades and tawny owls start to hoot from the trees. Moving through still night air without being able to see brings all your other senses alive. You'll be able to smell the plants and trees you pass and feel the pockets of warm and cool air; suddenly sounds will magnify, from the crunch of gravel underfoot and the rustle of leaves nearby to the music of a stream and the rush of the wind through the trees. Gradually, as your eyes allow, the stars glow brighter and more and more start to appear.

A moonless night somewhere where there's little light pollution makes for an incredible stellar display. When you remove the usual goals of a walk – destinations, speed, even the next hill – you experience a place in so much more detail. Ask children to talk about and

Enjoying the campfire at Highertown Campsite, Cornwall.

describe all the things they can see, feel, hear and smell – help them to identify things if they're not sure. Allow everyone to become accustomed to their reduced vision and bear in mind some people find it much harder to walk through darkness than others, so make sure you stay all together and don't rush anyone.

You can go on a night walk in many places – even wandering around a garden is exciting when it's dark. (Be sure to check the opening times of National Trust properties before you visit.) Night walking is a great adventure to combine with others, such as camping and sleeping outdoors. Here are some of our favourite places to immerse ourselves in the wonders of the night:

The beach – the sea sounds amazing at night; its rising and falling seems so much louder and more exciting than during the day with its many distractions. Penbryn Beach in Cardigan Bay is a wild and peaceful place to be at night, with very little light pollution and incredible views of the sky.

The woods – woodland comes alive at night with rustlings and hootings, and you can play hide-and-seek among the trees for even more excitement!

Mountains and moorland – for the best views of a star-filled sky open places are perfect for a night walk. Dartmoor and Exmoor in Devon; Mam Tor in the Peak District; Snowdonia and much of the Lake District and Northumberland are all wonderful places to watch the stars and experience the night-time world.

TOP TIPS

- Allow plenty of time for your eyes and other senses to adjust to the dark. It takes at least half an hour for your night vision to be at its best, so take your walk slowly to begin with.
- Take something to sit on with you on your walk; night-time can be dewy and cold so it's nice to have a warm, dry seat if you want to stop for a while.
- Leave glow sticks as you go so you can find your way back (make sure you pick them up on your return).
- Attach a small LED or head torch to younger children so you don't lose them in the dark!

GREAT FOR

NATURE • ACTIVE

Where to go

Dawn at Carding Mill Valley.

WEST MIDLANDS

The Long Mynd

Church Stretton, Shropshire SY6 6JG

Carding Mill Valley and the Long Mynd is a sweeping, heather-clad valley with a stream running through it. Perfect for cycling, walking, exploring and paddling, it's an ideal place for a day's family adventures. Once the sun sets it's also a great place for a night walk, listening to the night-time world awakening all around, or sitting peacefully at the water's edge and watching the stars fill the sky.

EAST OF ENGLAND

Sheringham Park

Upper Sheringham, Norfolk NR26 8TL

Sheringham Park feels wild and jungly, with its dense foliage of rhododendrons and azaleas and coastal woodland. The café and visitor centre close at 5pm, however the park is open until dark, when you'll see bats flitting through the air and hear the calls of owls. Or walk down to the sea and listen to its music – it's even more mesmerising in the dark.

Snow-covered branches at Sheringham Park, Norfolk.

SOUTH WEST

Highertown Farm

Lansallos, Looe, Cornwall PL13 2PX

Nestled within the peaceful Cornish village of Llansallos, Highertown Farm is a perfect place for a camping holiday filled with night-time adventures. Wander around the old buildings looking for bats and barn owls; head down the winding woodland path accompanied by the calls of tawny owls to reach the cove with its miniature waterfall; or simply sit outside your tent and let the night come to you.

5 Wildlife safari: parks and gardens

You don't need to venture far in order to have an amazing adventure when it comes to wildlife. It's there in every garden, park, grassy verge and leafy tree, and is often easy and rewarding to find, even for very small children. Get them to gently turn over a brick or a stone and see how many different creatures are making their homes underneath, from woodlice and worms to mites and millipedes. Pre-schoolers in particular are endlessly fascinated by these hidden worlds; so easily accessible, yet so different to their own home.

Parks and gardens – from the impressive landscaped ones to your very own back yard – are great places for wildlife watching. We keep a list of all the birds and butterflies we spot on adventures from our back door, either in the garden or in our local area. The variety is amazing and it's always exciting to add a new species to the ever-growing list.

Garden birds are a great place to start for younger children. Hang a bird

Watching the ducks at Colby Woodland Garden, Pembrokeshire.

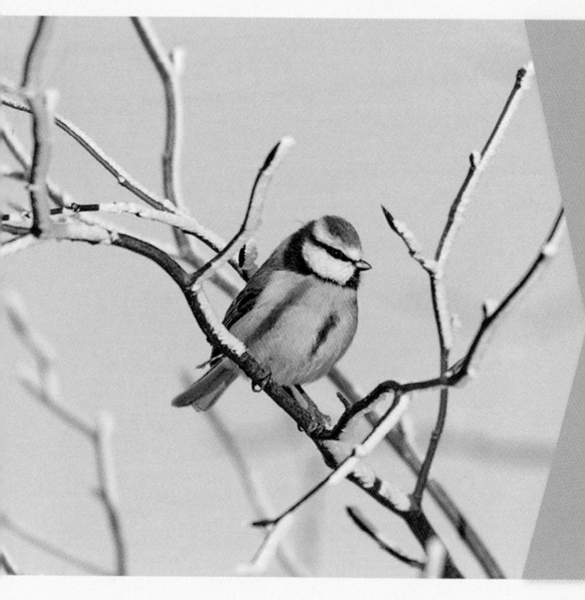

FUN FACTS

- There are around 250 species of bee in the UK: 24 species of bumblebee; around 225 species of solitary bee; and just a single honeybee species.
- Blue tits and great tits deliver around 10,000 caterpillars to their young each season.
- A blue tit weighs about the same as a pound coin.

A blue tit perches on a snowy branch.

feeder from a nearby tree; stuff an apple with seeds; put out a bird bath or a bird table and watch birds flock to your garden. Even a small patch of ground with the right things in it can be a haven for birds. If you have a bird table, set up a smartphone next to some food and video your feathered visitors: an easy way for kids to make a great little wildlife film of their own.

Butterflies are another exciting and rewarding creature that you'll find in gardens and local parks. Find the sorts of flowers they collect nectar from – buddleia is a common garden flower that's often covered with butterflies. Wildflowers will attract species such as speckled wood, gatekeeper and meadow brown, whereas peacocks, red admirals, small tortoiseshells and commas love stinging nettles. Bees will head for many of the same flowers too; if you have some garden to spare it's a great idea to plant some pollinator-friendly species and you'll be able to watch them visiting regularly to collect nectar. Many fruit, vegetable and herb plants are great for pollinators – and for us too.

Fortunately, many National Trust properties have glorious gardens filled with plants perfect for attracting insects. Great Chalfield Manor in Wiltshire is one of our favourites, with its large borders filled with a dazzling display of colourful flowers and rows of lavender that buzz with bees in the summer.

GREAT FOR YOUNGER KIDS • NATURE • ACTIVE

Spotting guide

ROBIN

BLACKBIRD

LADYBIRD

EARTH WORM

PEACOCK BUTTERFLY

RED ADMIRAL BUTTERFLY

SPIDER

NETTLE

DOCK LEAF

DAISY

DANDELION

BUMBLEBEE

Where to go

SOUTH EAST

Emmetts Garden

Ide Hill, Sevenoaks, Kent TN14 6BA

 (dogs on short leads)

This fascinating nineteenth-century garden contains many rare trees and shrubs from around the world and is great to explore. Follow the winding trails around the rock garden, discover the wild woodland and spot the abundant wildlife that makes its home here. One of the highest points in Kent, Emmetts Garden offers panoramic views over the surrounding Weald.

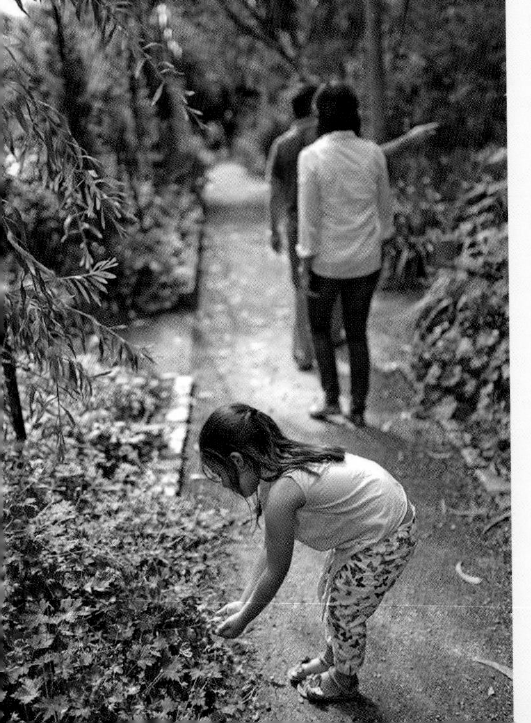

NORTHERN IRELAND

Mount Stewart

Portaferry Road, Newtownards, County Down BT22 2AD

Voted one of Britain's top 10 gardens, Mount Stewart is an astonishing example of experimental planting and design and also a fantastic place for kids to explore. Experience the Mediterranean feel of the formal gardens and the wild of the woods. Borrow a tracker pack, spot the animal sculptures and keep your eyes peeled for red squirrels.

Looking for wildlife at Mount Stewart, County Down.

Wildlife-attracting plants at Attingham Park, Shropshire.

WEST MIDLANDS

Attingham Park

Atcham, Shrewsbury, Shropshire SY4 4TP

   (park but not gardens)

Attingham is a haven for wildlife: insects buzz around the incredible walled garden; fallow deer and pedigree Jersey and Longhorn cattle graze the parkland; ravens and buzzards soar overhead. It's perfect for all types of wildlife safaris in this book, in fact, with ponds and woodland on the estate. There's a children's quiz trail and an activity room within the mansion.

Wildlife safari: woodland and forest

There's nothing like spending the day in the woods. Research – both scientific and anecdotal – has found that trees are good for all of us; even simply being able to see trees makes us happier. Woods and forests are a ready-made playground for children (and adults) of any age: climbing, playing with sticks, kicking through the leaves, balancing on logs, making dens – the list of potential activities is endless and unstructured, engaging creativity and inventiveness as well as physical activity. There's so much to see and do and all in an environment that we find at once exciting and calming.

A wildlife safari is a great way to get kids looking around them and naming the things that they see. It's empowering to know the different features, plants and creatures and even quite young children enjoy getting to grips with interesting-sounding names.

Woods are great places to spot birds, and they're often quite different from those found in gardens and urban areas. Start by listening to the birdsong, trying to identify some different sounds. Look up into the leafy canopy and you

FUN FACTS

- 12% of the UK is covered with trees, a level that has been steadily increasing over the past few decades.
- Trees create perfect habitats for hundreds of creatures, even when the tree is no longer alive.

Exploring the woodland around Killerton, Devon.

Looking into a badger set.

might see jays, thrushes and blackbirds; further up still are the circling birds of prey such as buzzards and hawks; search the tree trunks for woodpeckers, tree creepers and nuthatches; robins love to perch on fallen trees and dippers love woodland streams. See how many you can spot. The RSPB's online Bird Identifier is a great resource if you see any more unusual species. Woodland is also literally crawling with insects. Gently lift up a piece of dead wood and see what you can see underneath – woodlice and beetles perhaps. You might hear a dragonfly's distinctive rattling buzz as it 'hawks' past or find a delicate spider's web strung between branches. On a warm summer day you'll spot butterflies: look for pretty brown speckled woods, colourful peacocks or even rare white admirals. And then there are the mammals that make the forest their home: mice rustling through the leaves; acrobatic squirrels jumping from branch to branch; red and roe deer; bats; badgers; and – if you're very lucky – perhaps even a snoozing dormouse.

TOP TIPS

- Use a variety of methods to document your finds: drawings, photos, videos and sound recordings.
- Wildlife spotting is a great activity for afternoons once everyone's had plenty of time to run around. Sit in one spot and be as quiet as you can… What can you see?
- Don't worry if you can't name every species you see – take a photo or a description and look it up when you get home.
- Many National Trust places hold organised nature walks where you can learn from an expert as you go.

GREAT FOR

YOUNGER KIDS • NATURE • ACTIVE

Spotting guide

WOODPECKER

THRUSH

DEER

RABBIT

SQUIRREL

BAT

SPECKLED WOOD BUTTERFLY

OAK TREE

BEECH TREE

SYCAMORE TREE

WOODLOUSE

FUNGI

Where to go

SOUTH WEST

Ashclyst Forest

Killerton, Broadclyst, Devon EX5 3LE

On the edge of the Killerton Estate, a few miles from the main house and facilities, Ashclyst Forest is an enchanted place filled with ancient oaks and precious wildlife. The mixture of habitats supports a large number of butterflies, from the more common speckled woods and gatekeepers to rare white admirals and purple emperors. How many can you spot?

EAST OF ENGLAND

Hatfield Forest

Takeley, Bishop's Stortford, Essex CM22 6NE

A former royal hunting forest, Hatfield is a wonderful day out in the woods, just a short hop from London. Carefully managed for centuries, over 3,500 species of wildlife live here, some of which are rare and threatened. Keep an eye out for shy muntjac deer, woodland and water birds and the many insects who make their homes here. There's also a family trail and monthly children's clubs. Boat and all-terrain buggy hire available.

Fallow deer at Lyme, Cheshire.

The woodland at Doulaucothi Gold Mines.

WALES

Dolaucothi Estate

Pumsaint, Llanwrda, Carmarthenshire SA19 8US

Dolaucothi is most famous for its gold mining, a practice that took place here from Roman times until 1938. But its setting, among densely wooded hillside overlooking the Cothi Valley, makes it a perfect place to spot woodland wildlife. Follow the woodland trail, looking out for badgers and woodpeckers or head out on mountain bikes or horseback. The mines themselves are fascinating to visit and there are daily guided tours – or even have a go at panning for gold!

7 Wildlife safari: lakes and ponds

Lakes and ponds make fascinating habitats for all kinds of wildlife. Because they're often 'closed' bodies of water they evolve into an ecosystem where each creature and plant plays its own important part. Interestingly, fish are often bad for ponds as they eat the water plants that would otherwise provide shelter for other creatures and disturb the mud at the bottom of the pond, creating cloudy water in which other species struggle to survive.

Areas around lakes and ponds are often havens for wildlife, providing drinking water for animals such as deer and foxes and homes for the likes of ducks, herons and kingfishers, and it's always worth approaching slowly and quietly so you can spot any creatures in, on or around the water before they spot

Pond dipping at Hatfield Forest, Essex.

you. In early spring look out for spawn; frogspawn is laid in clumps whereas toads lay theirs in long chains. As the year progresses the tiny black dots will enlarge and become tadpoles, eventually turning into adult toads and frogs.

Pond dipping is a great way to take a closer look at some of the creatures living below the surface. You'll need a net to dip with and a shallow tray filled with water for observing your catch. Here are some tips for dipping success:

- Once you're at the water's edge, have a good look in to see where the best places to dip are.
- Carefully lower your net into the water and move it in a slow figure-of-eight motion. Repeat at different depths.
- Gently lift the net out and place it inside-out in your tray filled with water.
- Have a really good look at your findings – you could use a magnifying glass. How many of the creatures in the spotting guide (overleaf) can you see?
- Take photos or make notes on any creatures you find that you can't identify – you can always look them up when you get home.

TOP TIPS

- To go pond dipping you'll need a net. These are available in shops or you can make your own using a wire coat hanger and a muslin or an old pair of tights.
- Combine this wildlife safari with our Circumnavigate a Lake adventure (page 72) for twice the fun!

GREAT FOR

YOUNGER KIDS • NATURE • ACTIVE

Water wildlife hunting at Great Chalfield Manor, Wiltshire.

Looking for wildlife on Rothy Lake at Wallington, Northumberland.

Spotting guide

DUCK

HERON

GOOSE

DRAGONFLY

FROG

NEWT

POND SKATER

WATER SNAIL

FISH

WATER LILY

TOAD

DAMSEL FLY

Where to go

WALES

Bosherston Lily Ponds

The Old Home Farm Yard, Stackpole, Pembrokeshire SA71 5DQ

Bosherston Lakes, or lily ponds as they're commonly known, on the Stackpole Estate are large man-made lakes fed by natural springs. They're buzzing with wildlife and adorned with water lilies. There are also resident otters, which you might spot if you're lucky. Stackpole's stretch of stunning coastline is a hub for outdoor adventures, with sandy beaches, rock climbing, sea kayaking and coasteering to enjoy. You can stay onsite in one of the holiday cottages or there are several good campsites nearby (not National Trust).

Bosherton Lily Ponds.

WEST MIDLANDS

Dudmaston

Quatt, near Bridgnorth, Shropshire WV15 6QN

The gardens and orchard at Dudmaston are a brilliant exploring ground for children of all ages, and produce grown in the kitchen garden can be sampled in the tea room. Bigger adventures are to be found further into the estate, where Big Pool and Dingle Wood are waiting to be investigated for wildlife of all shapes and sizes. You'll also find lots of kid-friendly organised activities here, including woodland camps, guided bike rides and summer-holiday activity days.

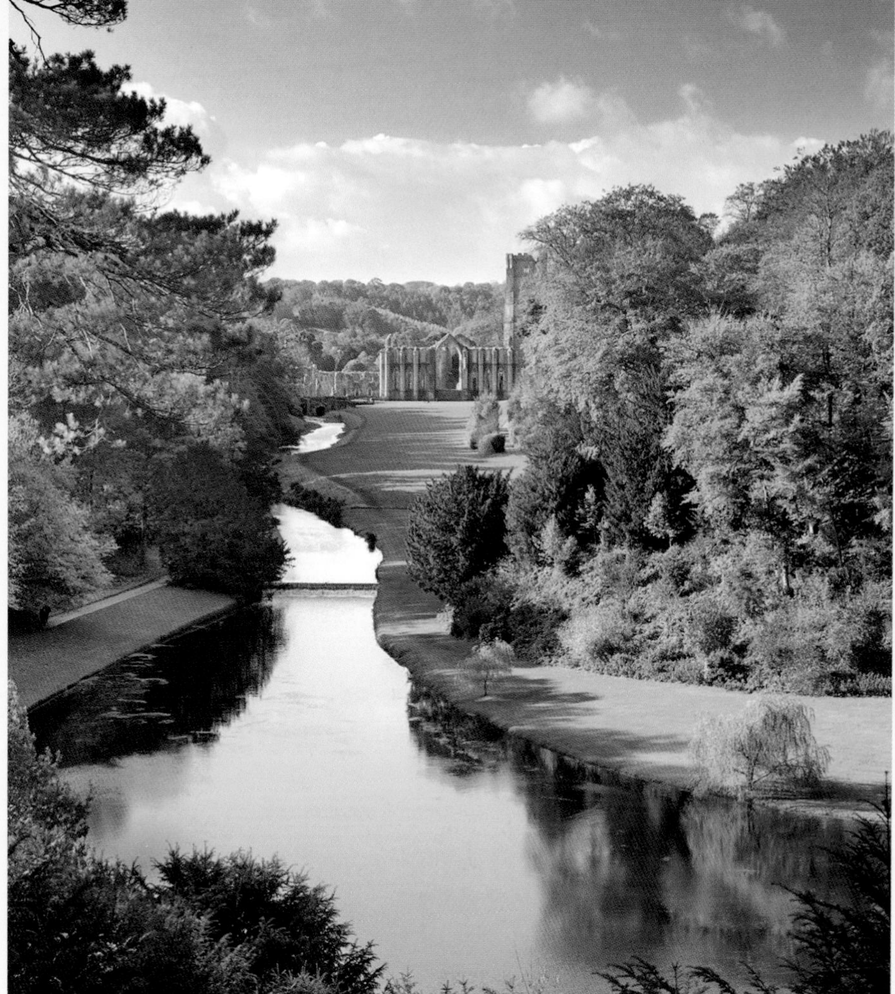

Looking over the Half Moon Pond at Studley Royal Water Garden.

NORTH

Fountains Abbey and Studley Royal Water Garden

Fountains, Ripon, North Yorkshire HG4 3DY

Recently recognised as a World Heritage Site, this is a special place indeed. The ruins of a beautiful Cistercian abbey rise above elegant Georgian water gardens, reflecting its character in more ways than one. It's a perfect place to spot pond life – there are organised pond-dipping sessions you can join – why not stop for a picnic on the riverside lawn and see what you can see?

8 Hunt for fossils

Just hearing the name of the Jurassic Coast conjures up images of prehistoric creatures and a whole different world from the one we know today. It does indeed feel like an otherworldly place in some respects, with its crumbling, rugged cliffs, undulating coast path and quiet, pebbly beaches. It's on these beaches that you'll make some wonderful discoveries if you look hard enough. We've spotted fragments of larger fossils; whole small creatures and shells and some beautiful ammonites, ridged and curled into tight spirals, set into the wave-washed limestone like carvings. One of our favourite places to go fossil-hunting is Burton Bradstock in Dorset which, millions of years ago, was a tropical sea and saltmarsh. As the land gradually shifted over the years the fossilised remains of the creatures that once lay on the sea floor are now visible in the cliffs and on the beaches.

Fossils can be found all over the UK and are an exciting discovery to make; imprints created millions of years ago in warm or frozen seas that have, through the passing of time, ended up scattered about for us to find. Because they're so old it's important that fossils remain where they're found for others to see and as a part of the historical record of a place. In general, don't damage or remove fossils – take a photo instead.

You don't even have to go out hunting for fossils to see some incredible examples. Arlington Court in Devon is home to two beautiful ammonites and Florence Court, in County Fermanagh, houses the Earl's fossil collection in the Rock Hound Room, with lots of activities.

You can even try making your own fossils. First collect some interesting leaves from the garden. Then take a small ball of air-dry clay and press it down over a leaf, making sure it completely covers it. Carefully turn the clay over and peel off the leaf: a homemade fossil! Once the fossils are dry you can paint them. Try using other things too, such as acorns or interesting-shaped stones.

Left: A child holds an ammonite fossil.
Right: Fossils on Dancing Ledge, Dorset.

GREAT FOR YOUNGER KIDS • NATURE • ACTIVE

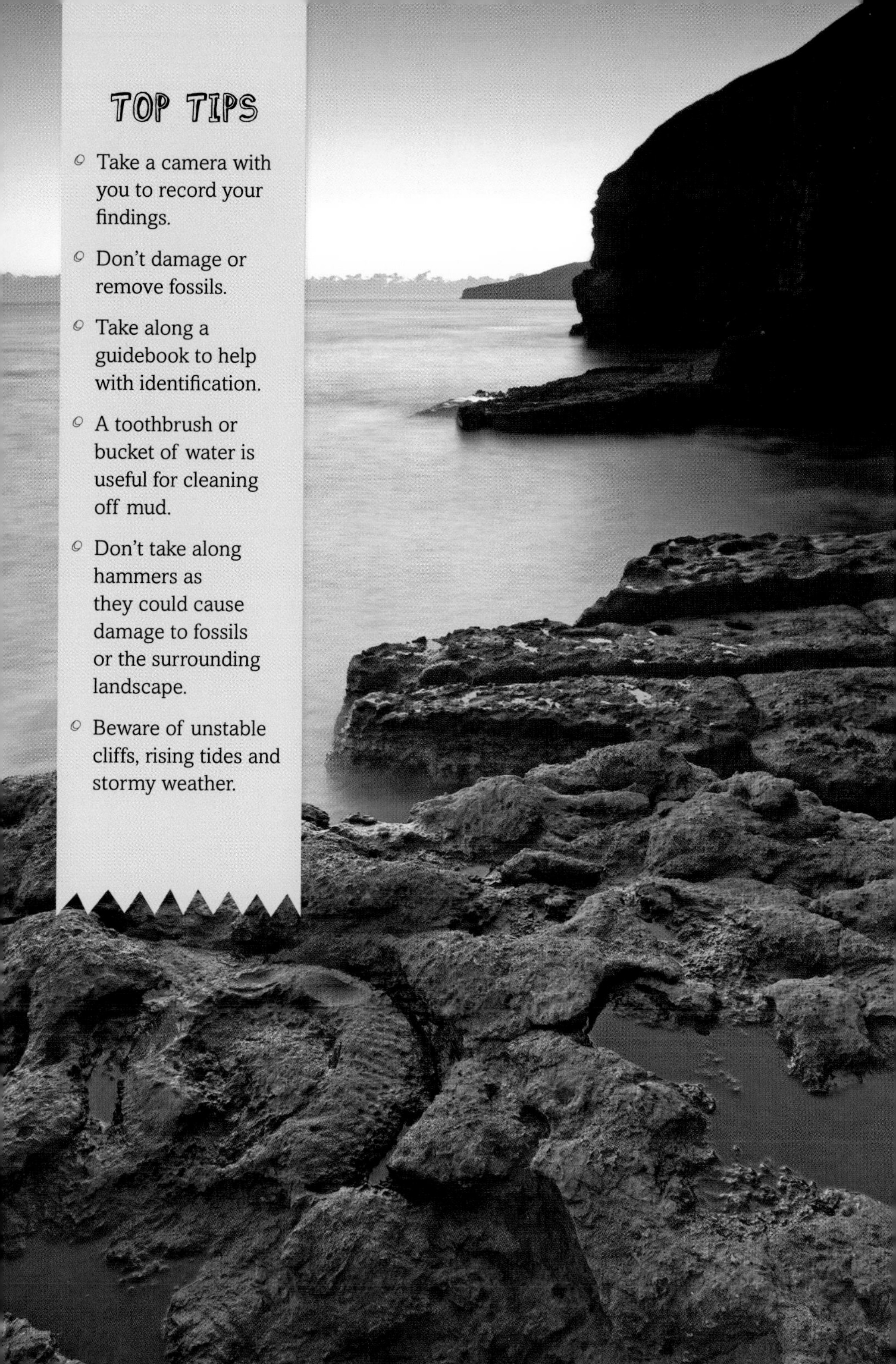

TOP TIPS

- Take a camera with you to record your findings.
- Don't damage or remove fossils.
- Take along a guidebook to help with identification.
- A toothbrush or bucket of water is useful for cleaning off mud.
- Don't take along hammers as they could cause damage to fossils or the surrounding landscape.
- Beware of unstable cliffs, rising tides and stormy weather.

Where to go

SOUTH WEST

- The Jurassic Coast, including Burton Bradstock and Charmouth, on the Golden Cap Estate

SOUTH EAST

- The chalk cliffs at Birling Gap, part of the Seven Sisters
- The Isle of Wight – sometimes referred to as 'dinosaur island' because it has so many fossils
- The chalk cliffs of the South Downs

NORTH EAST

- The East Yorkshire Coast is a great place to find fossils: visit Staithes, Port Mulgrave, Runswick, Robin Hood's Bay, Boggle Hole and Saltburn to see what treasures you can find

WALES

- Abereiddi, in Pembrokeshire, is famous for its graptolite fossils: the remains of colonies of tiny animals that lived in the sea up to 470 million years ago

NORTH WEST

- Arnside and Silverdale's limestone features in Cumbria
- Fossilised footprints on Formby Beach, Merseyside

EAST

- Head to Blakeney Point, Norfolk, to find washed-up fossils – sometimes even those of ammonites

NORTHERN IRELAND

- Recent findings at the Giant's Causeway, County Antrim, have included stromatolites, the oldest known fossils, made by primitive blue-green algae

Left: Fossil hunting on the Jurassic Coast.
Right: Ammonite fossils.

9 A winter beach adventure

The beach is a universally popular destination when the sun's hot and the sea's invitingly cool. But our favourite time of year for a beach holiday is in the depths of winter when the crowds have vanished and the sea comes to life with big waves that crash onto the rocks, filling the air with salty spray. There's nothing like wrapping up warm and battling the wind for a walk along a deserted beach; skimming stones across foaming white water; building sandcastles with your gloves on or paddling in wellies and a toasty pair of socks. And then, of course, there's heading inside at the end of the day to warm up in front of a roaring fire.

Crisp, cold winter weather is wonderful at the beach and, with a little planning, can make for a full day of family adventuring. We pack up our trusty Kelly

Playing on the dunes at Formy, near Liverpool.

FUN FACTS

- The National Trust looks after more than 775 miles (1,247km) of Britain's beautiful coastline.
- Including all its principal islands, the coast of Britain stretches a massive 19,491 miles (31,368km).

Making sandcastles in Devon.

kettle, with its many dents from years of camping trips. It has a metal base, in which you light a fire, and a cylindrical water container with a hole all the way through the middle. Pop the container on top of the fire and in a few minutes you'll have enough hot water for drinks for everyone. The kids love foraging for firewood, finding dry sticks and pieces of driftwood to keep the flames burning, and it's a lovely thing to sit around the fire together, hands warming around a steaming mug of tea.

It's worth embracing the emptiness of British beaches at this time of year too: see how many sandcastles you can build in a line; write poetry in the sand; create works of art with shells, seaweed and driftwood; or simply enjoy running around uninhibited by crowds of sunbathers.

Accommodation near the beach is often more affordable during the winter months. The National Trust has some amazing properties right on the coast where you can watch the stormy waves from the warmth of your front room. Or, if you're feeling like a wilder adventure, you could even camp…

TOP TIPS

- If you're taking a Kelly/storm kettle or other solid-fuel cooker with you, take along some dry kindling to get the fire going.
- If you're thinking of paddling – or even swimming – a winter wetsuit and/or neoprene shoes can make the experience much more bearable. There are many organised Christmas, Boxing Day and New Year swims (not National Trust) throughout the country.

GREAT FOR YOUNGER KIDS • NATURE • ACTIVE

Where to go

SOUTH WEST

Holywell and Crantock

Cornwall TR8 5PF (Holywell), TR8 5RN (Crantock)

(not National Trust) (not National Trust)

A glorious, golden crescent of sand awaits adventure in this relatively quiet part of the north Cornish coast, just a few miles from busy Newquay. The warmer climate makes it perfect for winter adventures, and sand is a great alternative to mud when it comes to digging holes.

The impressive Gull Rocks at Holywell Bay.

WALES

Rhossili

Swansea SA3

(not National Trust) (not National Trust)

Three miles (nearly 5km) of golden sand edge this beautiful part of the Gower Peninsula. Bordered by rocky outcrops and the windswept hills of Rhossili Down, this is a perfect place to play at any time of year. At low tide you can spot the remains of the ship the *Helvetia*, wrecked here in 1887. The open expanse of Rhossili also makes it a perfect place for flying kites.

NORTHERN IRELAND

Portstewart Strand

118 Strand Road, Portstewart, County Londonderry BT55 7PG

 (not National Trust) 

Considered one of Northern Ireland's finest beaches, Portstewart is arguably even better in winter, when the crowds have vanished and you have the place to yourself. Two miles (over 3km) of sand edge the coast with fine views and lots to see and do nearby. The area is a haven for wildlife, with a bird sanctuary, walks around the conservation site and – in summertime – a colourful collection of wild flowers and butterflies.

Exploring the sand dunes at Portstewart Strand.

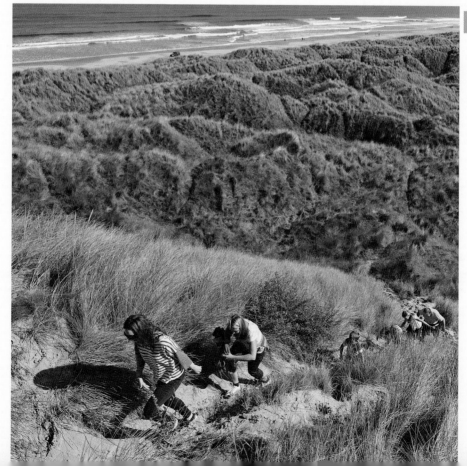

10 Celebrate a festival

A festival of apples: wassailing and Apple Day

Children and orchards simply go together: picking apples, climbing trees, playing tag and picnics in the grass all make for some wonderful family days out. The National Trust has more than 309 acres of traditional orchard and apple events are gaining in popularity every year. They're also a great way to learn about caring for orchards, and the vast number of apple varieties to be found.

Wassailing is an ancient tradition from the apple-producing regions of Britain, particularly the South West. Originally a ceremony to 'bless' the trees in the hope of encouraging them to produce a bountiful crop later in the year, wassails have now become a celebration of the orchards and an appreciation of the need to conserve them for future generations, as well as an opportunity for communities to share an evening of revelry. Expect dancing, lantern-making, tree-climbing, local bands and plenty of food and drink for all to enjoy. The tradition is spreading, and each year more places are including wassailing in their calendar, often combined with Christmas festivities.

- There are hundreds of family-friendly festivals across Britain, celebrating everything from books and music to kites and kayaks. The National Trust hosts some great festivals throughout the year; our favourites are listed on page 62.

Picking apples at Parke, Devon.

Apple pressing on Apple Day at Parke, Devon.

Apple Day, 21 October, is a project set up by environmental charity Common Ground in 1990 to bring communities together to celebrate and conserve the incredible richness and diversity of, not just apples, but also the local landscape, ecology and culture. Volunteers are on-hand to help with apple-related craft activities and you can get involved in harvesting the apples, tasting the different varieties straight from the tree, loading buckets for ponies to carry or helping with the cider press and sampling the freshest juice you can imagine.

TOP TIPS

- Festivals are busy and it's easy to get separated from family members – pre-arrange a place to meet up and give younger children wristbands with your mobile number on.
- Camping is an enjoyable part of many festivals. If you can, pitch away from floodlights and generators so you wake refreshed and ready to have fun.

GREAT FOR

YOUNGER KIDS • NATURE • ACTIVE • FOOD & DRINK • 50 THINGS

Where to go

SOUTH WEST

- Killerton Cider and Apple festival, Devon, in October. This festival celebrates all things apples, with apple picking, pressing and tasting and lots of other family-friendly activities.
- South West Outdoor Festival. Held in a variety of stunning locations around the south west each September, SWOF combines family-friendly activities with sporting events, plus lots of inspiring talks from leading adventurers.

NORTH WEST

- Keswick Mountain Festival is held in June each year on the banks of beautiful Derwent Water, with views out across the lake to Catbells. It's an exciting mix of adventure, music, events and activities suitable for all ages. The festival also raises much-needed funds for the National Trust's conservation work in the area.

WALES

- Stackpole Sea Kayaking Festival, Pembrokeshire in May. Immerse yourself in the stunning surroundings of the Stackpole Estate and enjoy a weekend of guided trips and excursions, live music and inspiring speakers. There's full catering all weekend, including packed lunches to take exploring.

NORTHERN IRELAND

- Kite Festival at Downhill Demesne. Each August hundreds of kites of all shapes, sizes and colours take to the skies above this glorious coastal estate. There's entertainment all day long with kite-making, stunt demos and food and craft stalls.

EAST OF ENGLAND

- Castaway weekend camping festival, Northey Island, in July. Escape to Northey Island in Essex, walking across the causeway or arriving by boat at high tide, for a weekend of family camping fun. Expect lots of organised activities for all ages and great evening entertainment.

Celebrating Christmas at Buckland Abbey, Devon.

11 Take a boat trip

Boats and water are inherently exciting and, as a mode of transport, entirely different from that which most of us are used to. Boat trips can be big or small, gentle or adventurous, but always a fun and popular family day out.

The National Trust looks after many stretches of precious coastline in the North East of England, including castles, lighthouses, the abundance of wildlife and the 15–20 (depending upon the tide) wild and windswept Farne Islands and Lindisfarne, with its dramatic castle perched high on a rocky outcrop, fascinating history and tidal causeway. The Farne Islands are home to seals, puffins and over 100,000 seabirds, making them a brilliant place to spot wildlife.

The Farne Islands are only accessible by boat from nearby Seahouses. Boat trips vary in length, from a couple of hours' touring around the islands, stopping close enough to get a great view but staying in the boat, to longer trips that give you the opportunity to

TOP TIPS

- Pick a boat trip of a duration that will work for your child's age – younger children may be happier on shorter trips or those where you can stop regularly, whereas older children will be happier being aboard for longer.
- Adding in a boat trip can be a great way of making a walk more exciting. The Lake District is a perfect place for this as many of the lakes have steamers operating. Why not walk halfway around the lake and then jump on the boat home?

Watching seals at Blakeney Point, Norfolk.

GREAT FOR **WILDLIFE •YOUNGER CHILDREN • WATER**

get out and walk about on some of the islands. We chose the first option, packing plenty of food to keep the kids warm and occupied. It was exciting, climbing into the little boat, which rocked gently on the choppy water, and heading off towards the distant islands.

The seabirds here are incredible, from gannets that fall from the sky like arrows to the puffins that zoom around like tiny clown-faced speedboats. The many nesting birds on the rocks at first look like a jumble of white but, as you approach and under the expertise of the boat crew, they become a fascinating array of species, all easily identifiable once the differences have been pointed out.

A boat trip is a great way to explore a river, seeing a place from a different perspective. At Cliveden in Buckinghamshire, inspiration for Kenneth Grahame's classic *The Wind in the Willows* tales and one of the prettiest stretches of the River Thames, you can jump aboard a cruiser and relax for a guided tour of the river. Or, if you'd prefer to be skipper to your own adventure for the day, pack a picnic and head out in a classic rowing or self-drive motorboat. Or use a boat trip to start a bigger adventure, like jumping aboard one of the small ferries across Poole Harbour to Brownsea Island in Dorset, where deer, peacocks and red squirrels run wild; or across the glorious River Dart in Devon to Greenway, Agatha Christie's holiday hideaway.

Above: Boating on the River Wey, Surrey.

11
Take a boat trip

Where to go

SOUTH EAST

Dapdune Wharf Navigations Office

Wharf Road, Guildford, Surrey GU1 4RR

Twenty miles (32km) of tranquil waterway – one of the first rivers in Britain to be made navigable – run through the heart of Surrey. Boat trips on quiet electric launches run from Thursday to Monday during open season and all week in August. The trips last for about 40 minutes and take in some of the best bits of the river, with wildlife and history all around. You can also kayak and navigate your own boat.

Learning about pulleys at Dapdune Wharf.

The ferry to Greenway.

SOUTH WEST

Greenway

Greenway Road, Galmpton, near Brixham, Devon TQ5 0ES

(garden only)

Travelling to Greenway on a boat up the River Dart is all part of the adventure. Jump on one of the hourly ferries from the bustling coastal town of Dartmouth; or make your way to the pretty village of Dittisham, where you can ring a bell and summon an open wooden boat to transport you across. There's an enjoyable winding walk up through the woods from the private quay to the house. You can also arrive by steam train.

Blakeney National Nature Reserve

Morston Quay, Quay Road, Morston, Norfolk NR25 7BH

(not National Trust) (not National Trust) at certain times

The 4-mile (6.5km) shingle spit of Blakeney Point protects this precious area from the sea, creating a haven for a vast array of wildlife. The grey seals are a particular highlight, and the best way to see them is by ferry from Morston Quay. There's a range of companies offering regular trips, or you can jump aboard with a National Trust Ranger at certain times of year for a guided tour.

Boats at Morston Quay, Blakeney.

12 A barefoot adventure

Cragside in Northumberland was the first house in the world to be lit by hydroelectric power. It's a fascinating place that pays testament to the creativity, eccentricity and genius of former owner, Lord Armstrong. At the top of the estate in Crozier car park lies the Barefoot Walk – kick off your shoes and prepare to get muddy as you complete the trail and discover the different textures of nature in between your toes. Don't worry, there's a tap at the end for you to wash off your feet – just remember to bring a towel!

You don't have to go on an 'official' walk of course, and being barefoot is a lovely way to make a family walk really different. The soles of our feet are covered with nerve endings, meaning they're highly sensitive to touch and going barefoot makes a walk interactive and interesting. Try some of the following things to walk on:

Sand – feel it sink under your weight; feel the difference between dry sand and wet sand; stand in the sand at the edge of the sea and feel what happens as the waves wash over – and under – your feet.

Shingle – coarser than sand but finer than pebbles, shingle shifts constantly as you walk but fills in your footprints afterwards.

Pebbles – smooth, round and wonderful for curling your toes around, pebbles come in all sorts of shapes and sizes, colours and patterns. They make a lovely sound as they roll too.

Rocks – feeling your way across rocks in bare feet is fun and it's a great challenge to jump between them. It's a completely different experience from scrambling in shoes and you really get to feel the difference in texture between the different

TOP TIPS

- Check feet before and after the walk to make sure there aren't any cuts or grazes that need attending to.
- Check the ground you're going to be walking on for sharp and other unpleasant items.
- Make sure you're prepared with water and a towel to wash and dry everyone's feet when you're done.

rock types, from smooth, rounded gritstone to the edges and ledges of limestone and granite's sharp crystals.

Grass – the feeling of running barefoot on soft, springy grass is hard to beat. Moss underfoot adds cushioning, whereas long, coarse grass almost squeaks as you walk.

Mud – deep mud can be utterly joyful to squelch through barefoot. Leave your laundry concerns behind and feel the mud squidge between your toes.

Another great little adventure is to make your own sensory walk, adding whatever you can find to make it interesting underfoot: twigs, stepping stones, logs – anything you like that might be interesting to stand on. Take it in turns to walk around it, paying attention to what you feel. You could even try it blindfolded!

Left: Walking barefoot on the grass at Birling Gap, East Sussex. Below: Pebbles underfoot.

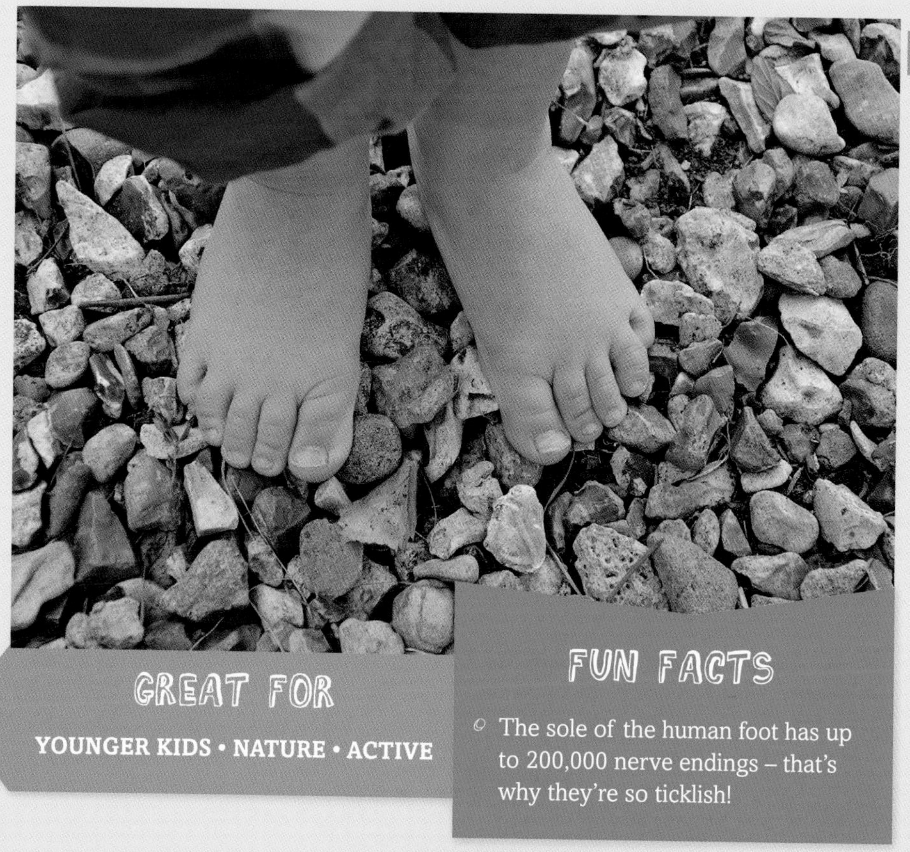

GREAT FOR

YOUNGER KIDS • NATURE • ACTIVE

FUN FACTS

- The sole of the human foot has up to 200,000 nerve endings – that's why they're so ticklish!

Where to go

NORTH EAST

Cragside

Rothbury, Morpeth, Northumberland
NE65 7PX

Cragside is filled with remnants of the genius of its former resident, Lord Armstrong. The gardens, including a huge rock garden, are exciting for all the family to explore and there's a labyrinth and dedicated barefoot trail.

EAST OF ENGLAND

Dunwich Beach

Dunwich, Saxmundham, Suffolk IP17 3DJ

Sometimes wild places can be a worry if you're taking a baby along, but Dunwich is brilliantly set up for families with children of any age. There's even a children's menu in the café. The beach is perfect for a barefoot exploration, with soft sand, rounded pebbles, dry or slimy seaweed and cold sea!

SOUTH WEST

Godolphin

Godolphin Cross, Helston, Cornwall TR13 9RE

Godolphin boasts some of the best views in Cornwall: south across to St Michael's Mount and north to the startlingly blue St Ives Bay. From mysterious woodland to riverside trails there's so much here to encourage families to immerse themselves in nature… including the dedicated barefoot trail and outdoor mud kitchen.

Cragside house, Northumberland.

13 Circumnavigate a lake

Walking at the lake at Stowe, Buckinghamshire.

It's really satisfying to set out on an adventure that is an obvious challenge – such as making your way around a lake – and completing it. For children in particular the ability to monitor their progress and see how far there is still to go gives them a level of control they'll relish.

There are so many lakes in Britain that provide wonderful places to spend the day: walking, picnicking, cycling, paddling and exploring by boat – activities suitable for families of all ages and abilities, often in beautiful surroundings. One of our favourites has to be the Lake District's Tarn Hows, not far from Coniston and formerly owned by Beatrix Potter. The trail around the tarn is a little under 2 miles (3.2km) and gently undulating, perfect for little legs. The path is well maintained and ideal for bikes, buggies and wheelchairs too. You're spoiled for choice when it comes to picnic spots: the whole place is beautiful, tranquil and abundant with wildlife, with majestic views out over the surrounding mountains. We spent another brilliant day at Cragside in the heart of Northumberland, walking around the picturesque lakes on the 1½-mile (2.4km) Nelly Moss Lakes Walk. All of the trails are

Exploring the lake at Stourhead, Wiltshire.

well signposted here, and the landscape and foliage creates an adventurous place to explore. It's particularly spectacular in summer when the rhododendrons are in bloom, providing colour and shade as you go. Cragside is a magical place for children: explore the labyrinth, looking out for William the Wizard and other sculptures; visit the young engineer's centre; or jump on the zip wire in the adventure playground.

Another great place for cycling, especially for those still mastering the skill, is Stowe in Buckinghamshire, with its beautiful Palladian bridge that spans a lake bustling with geese, ducks and moorhens. There are three trails of varying – but very achievable – distances that take you on a great adventure through the rolling 'Capability' Brown landscape.

TOP TIPS

- Travelling around a lake can be a gentle stroll or a day-long adventure – there are so many to choose from that there's always a new adventure to be found.
- Combine your walk with some other activities: go for a paddle or a sail a raft; spot wildlife on, in or around the water – or jump on a boat to see the shore from a different perspective.
- Lakes are often bigger than they look! Make sure you know how far it is all the way around before you set out.
- Pack a picnic to enjoy at a spot along the way – and get the kids to carry their own snacks if they'd like to.

GREAT FOR

YOUNGER KIDS • BUGGIES • NATURE • ACTIVE

Of course you don't have to travel around the lake on dry land – swimming along the shoreline is an exciting way to explore from a different perspective. Many lakes have boats available to hire – an exciting way to explore – or go for a paddle if it's shallow.

13
Circumnavigate a lake

Where to go

SOUTH WEST

Stourhead

near Mere, Wiltshire BA12 6QF

(dogs at certain times)

Stourhead manages perfectly to balance grandeur and formality with relaxation and accessibility. It really is a beautiful place to be, walking among splendidly landscaped gardens around the magnificent lake. And yet everywhere there's a sense of fun that connects with children: classical temples, strange caves and mystical grottoes. There's also the 2,650-acre estate to explore, where chalk downs, ancient woods and farmland are managed for wildlife.

SOUTH EAST

Stowe

Buckingham, Buckinghamshire MK18 5EQ

There's a delightful 3-mile (4.8km) cycle ride around the lake at Stowe: perfect for those just finding their pedals. There's so much to see and do: temples to explore; trees to climb; and landscaped valleys to run along. It's a great place for kids, with toddler sessions, weekend/summer holiday activities and a play area in the café – so you can relax for a moment with a good coffee.

Left: Glorious views of the lake at Stourhead, Wiltshire.

NORTH WEST

Derwent Water

near Keswick, Cumbria CA12 5DQ

Borrowdale and Derwent Water are a splendid destination for any family adventure. The recently launched, fully waymarked 10-mile (16km) route is an excellent challenge for families with older children who are up for a full day's walking – please note there are some short sections of road. There's a leaflet with full route details available online or at the National Trust shop and information centre on Keswick foreshore. Great things to spot include the beautiful mountains of Blencathra and Skiddaw, red squirrels and waterfowl as you cross the boardwalk over the wetlands.

Enjoying the space at Stowe, Buckinghamshire.

14 A wild weather adventure

On cold, grey days when the rain is lashing at the windows and the wind is buffeting the trees it can be tempting to hide indoors. But some of the most rewarding adventures can be found out and about in stormy weather – and a steaming mug of hot chocolate always tastes so much better when you've spent the day battling the elements. We spent a wonderful week exploring the Lake District as heavy snow fell in late April. The wind whipped up the surface of the water and sent snowflakes scudding across the ground. We had an unexpected wild weather adventure.

As long as they stay warm and fed, children are surprisingly robust when it comes to Great British Weather. Rain is for catching on your tongue or making puddles for splashing in; snow is for building snow creatures and throwing snowballs; wind is for kite flying and running around pretending you're an aeroplane… Here are some of our favourite wild weather adventures:

Scrambling up the path beside Stickle Ghyll, Cumbria.

GREAT FOR NATURE • ACTIVE • YOUNGER CHILDREN

Build a rain shelter

Build a simple den using long sticks to make the frame, either in a tepee or a tent shape. In summer, weave in leafy branches to make a roof or in winter use a tarpaulin to keep the rain out.

Go ice skating

There aren't many natural lakes that freeze enough to skate on in the UK, but large puddles are great fun to slide about on, or to spin pieces of ice, sticks or stones along. **Never venture onto frozen water if you don't know how thick it is.**

Cook up a storm in a mud kitchen

Younger children love playing with mud and pretending to cook too. Provide bowls and wooden spoons and get them making mud pies.

Make your own wind chime

A great activity for a beach holiday when the weather isn't quite Mediterranean... Collect a bucketful of thin, flat shells – clam or small scallop shells are perfect for this. Make a small hole in the pointed end of each one and thread onto a piece of ribbon – one for each shell. Attach the ribbons to a piece of driftwood and hang this in a breezy position where your shells will make a lovely tinkling sound every time the wind blows.

Of course, lots of our adventures are even better with a bit of wild weather: try flying a kite in the wind (page 128); walking barefoot through mud and rain (page 68); sledging in the snow (page 124); or brewing up on the beach (page 56). Wild swimming in the rain is a joy, too (page 192).

Family fun in the snow on Dartmoor, Devon.

TOP TIPS

- Kids warm up and cool down rapidly so take plenty of layers of clothing – plus spares for afterwards!
- Invest in a good set of waterproofs so you can let the children get on with getting wet and muddy.
- Take plenty of snack foods to keep energy levels up.
- Take a camera with you – it's tempting to leave it behind but you often get some of the best pictures on stormy days.

14
A wild weather adventure

Where to go

SOUTH WEST

Wellington Monument

Wellington, Somerset TA21 9PB

A tribute to the Duke of Wellington and his victory at the Battle of Waterloo, Wellington Monument stands on top of Wellington Hill, on the edge of the Blackdown Hills. It's visible from the M5 as you drive past on your way elsewhere, but it's a great place for an adventure and, the wilder the weather, the better! It's less than a mile (1.6km) from the National Trust car park to the summit and back but well worth the effort. Make sure you take your kite along too.

Splashing along the track at Box Hill, Surrey.

NORTH WEST

Tarn Hows

near Coniston, Cumbria LA21 8AG

Tarn Hows, given to the National Trust by Beatrix Potter, is a perfect place to visit at any time of year. There's a gently undulating walk of a little under 2 miles (3.2km) that makes its way around the Tarn, taking in exciting wooded areas, glorious views and even an orienteering course. Parking is nearby and a level walk away and the whole circuit is buggy-friendly. Please note: there is no cycling around Tarn Hows.

SOUTH EAST

Box Hill

Tadworth, Surrey KT20 7LB

Just a short hop from London, and with its own train station, Box Hill is a perfect destination for a wild and windy winter-weather adventure. There are lots of walks to try, each with points of interest and great views of the surrounding North Downs countryside. And there's no better way to celebrate a successful summit than with a hot chocolate in the café. Organised, family-friendly activities throughout the year.

A wild weather walk at Tarn Hows, Cumbria.

15 Watch the sunrise

In our busy lives it's tempting to feel that early mornings are best avoided, but when there's no rush-hour train journey, no school run to do or desk to sit at, but just the gradual awakening of the natural world to appreciate, watching the sun rise on a new day can be magical.

Kids are often surprisingly keen when it comes to an early morning expedition. For younger children simply sitting in the garden or by an open window watching and listening as the day arrives to the incredible sound of the dawn chorus is an adventure in its own right. It's great to set some time aside throughout the year to watch the differences: winter sunrises give you more of a lie-in but can be chilly, whereas summer tends to be warmer but means a much earlier start.

A great time to appreciate the sunrise is when you're camping (page 150). There's that first hint of light on the canvas. Then the birds start to sing, sensing that daybreak isn't far away. If you're pitched in one of the National Trust's many spectacular campsite locations, now's the time to exit the tent and immerse yourself in the fresh, early morning air. Wrap up warm, watch the sun paint a rainbow across the sky, then head back to the tent for breakfast. Even better, on a warm, summer morning, pack a picnic breakfast and take it with you.

Sunrise at Blickling Estate, Norfolk.

We've seen some spectacular sunrises over the sea on England's east coast, with the vast beaches and open skies of Norfolk and Northumberland being the best we've found. Watching the sun as it seems to rise straight out of the sea, its reflection turning the waves red and gold, is the perfect start to a day on the beach. Ancient sites – such as the standing stones at Avebury in Wiltshire – and ruined buildings like Corfe Castle in Dorset always feel even more special as the sun's first rays illuminate them.

If you have older children who are happy walking a few miles you could even join in one of the Early Morning Madness events, held in the summer at some locations. Starting at 3am there's a walk into the hills before settling down to watch the sunrise, followed by a well-earned breakfast.

Dawn at St Margaret's Bay, Dover, Kent.

GREAT FOR

YOUNGER CHILDREN • NATURE • ACTIVE

TOP TIPS

- If you can, get out when it's still completely dark, just as the first birds begin to sing.
- Take warm clothes and something warm to sit on.
- Take a camera: early morning is the best time to get some great shots.

15
Watch the sunrise

Where to go

Sunrise is best when you have uninterrupted views to the east, so you can catch it right from its very beginnings through – if you're lucky enough to be treated to a good one – to the moment when the whole sky fills with colour. Moorland, mountain, downland and levels are all great places to set up camp – in fact camping is one of the best ways to make sure you're there, ready for the first rays of the day. Coastal locations are particularly dramatic, as the sun appears to rise out of the sea. Some of the best places we've been fortunate to catch a beautiful sunrise are:

Avebury, Wiltshire
Druridge Bay, Northumberland
The White Cliffs of Dover, Kent
Ventnor Downs, Isle of Wight
Marsden Moor, West Yorkshire
Lizard Point, Cornwall
Dunwich Beach, Suffolk
Brecon Beacons, Powys
Carding Mill Valley, Shropshire

A misty morning at Avebury Stone Circle, Wiltshire.

16 A literary adventure

Beatrix Potter had an incredible gift: the gift of being able to connect deeply with children. She knew how to intrigue them, how to stimulate their imaginations and show them friendship, adventure, frustration and sometimes even fear through her characters. Hill Top, the house where she wrote many of her most treasured stories, is a cottage in Near Sawrey, just outside Hawkshead in the Lake District. It's not large or grand in any way, with its dark wood panelling and creaky staircase, but it's a real experience to visit, just as much for kids as for adults. We arrived at Hill Top in late April in a week of wintery weather. Snow covered the distant mountains and heavy sleet fell as we made our way up the lane and through the garden – one tended for Beatrix by the Girl Guides as she wasn't keen on gardening herself – and in through the little wooden door. Here you're presented with a couple of the author's iconic books and that's when the place really comes to life: that's the very door in one picture; the staircase in another with the same grandfather clock in the corner; there's the chimney that Tom Kitten escaped up – and the doll's house where the Two Bad Mice had their disappointing tea party. Left as if the owner has just popped out to tend her famous Herdwick sheep, it's an interesting and intriguing place that offers a fascinating insight into the mind of one of children's literature's best-loved people.

Long after we had finished spotting the various things we remembered from the books we've known all our lives, our daughter – aged 4 – was still standing by the doll's house, fascinated by its contents. She wanted to explore the house again and again; the place, even long after Beatrix Potter's departure, still a testament to Beatrix's uncanny ability to engage the child's mind.

On a brighter day there's much to explore nearby – a celebration of

FUN FACTS

- As a child, Beatrix Potter loved reading. She was inspired by many books, including *The Water Babies* by Charles Kingsley, Edward Lear's *Book of Nonsense*, *Alice in Wonderland* by Lewis Carroll and the *Brer Rabbit* stories by Joel Chandler Harris.
- In 2016 the first National Trust Children's Book Festival was held at Wray Castle in Cumbria – a celebration of the writers and illustrators that inspire and delight our children.

Beatrix's conservation work and legacy to the National Trust. When she died in 1943, she left 4,000 acres of land and countryside to the National Trust, as well as 14 farms, which are still managed in accordance with her wishes. Visit the gallery in Hawkshead where her original artwork is on display; walk around tranquil Tarn Hows (page 72); or dress up as a knight at Wray Castle (page 97).

Right: Climbing on Windermere's shore, Cumbria.
Below: Rudyard Kipling's desk at Bateman's, East Sussex.

GREAT FOR

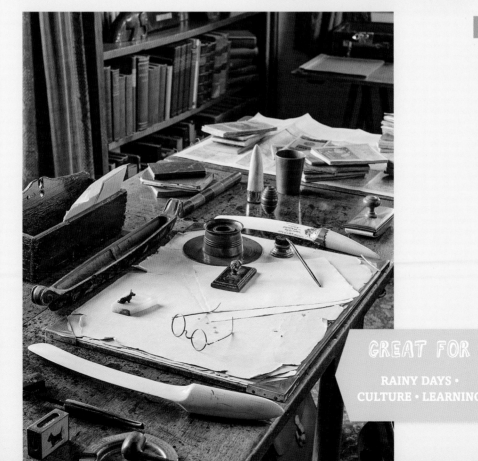

RAINY DAYS • CULTURE • LEARNING

Where to go

NORTH WEST

Hill Top

Near Sawrey, Hawkshead, Ambleside, Cumbria LA22 0LF

 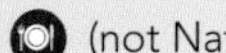 (not National Trust)

A fascinating time capsule of Beatrix Potter's life, from walking up through the pretty garden – a jumble of flowers, fruit and vegetables (is that a rabbit nibbling the lettuces?) – to the tiny interior where you can spot so many sources of inspiration. Food is available at the nearby Sawrey House Hotel or Tower Bank Arms (not National Trust). Entry to the house is by timed-ticket so there may be a wait.

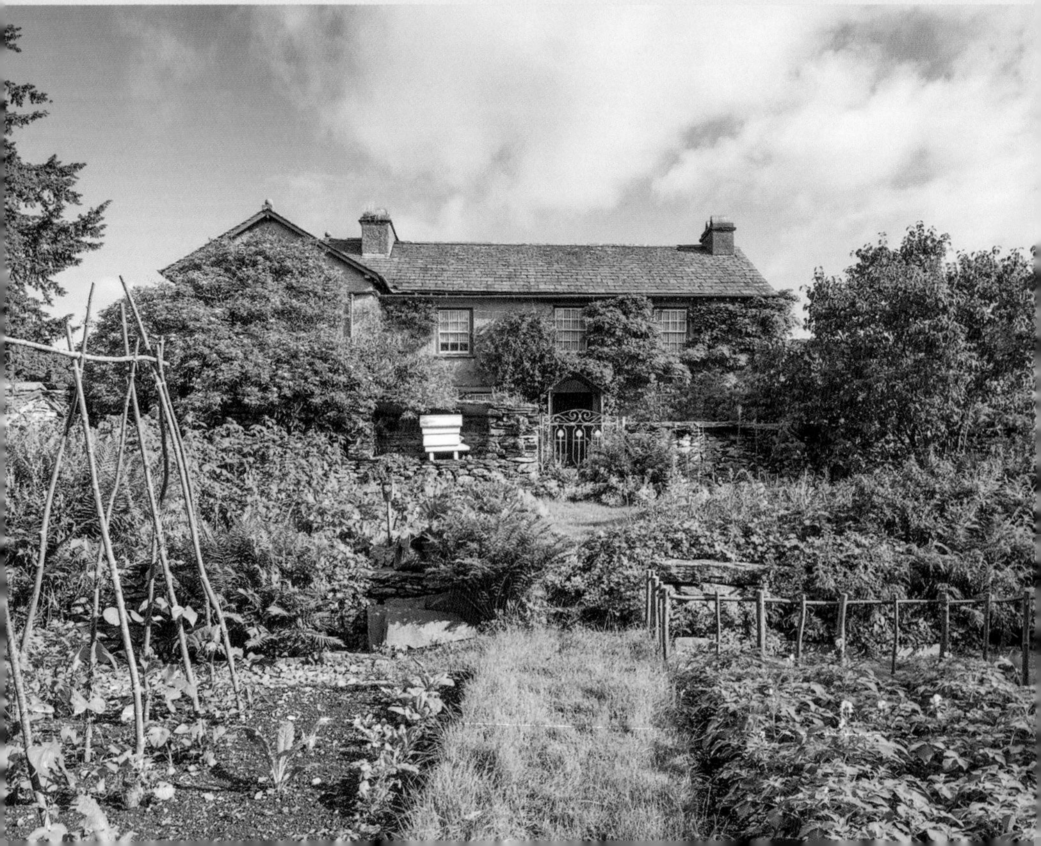

NORTH WEST

Windermere and Coniston

Cumbria

Arthur Ransome used several places in the Lake District as settings for his wonderful children's adventure books, *Swallows and Amazons*. According to Ransome, every place in his book can be found in the Lake District, but not necessarily as it originally appears: the lake is based on Windermere but the surrounding countryside is more similar to that around Coniston.

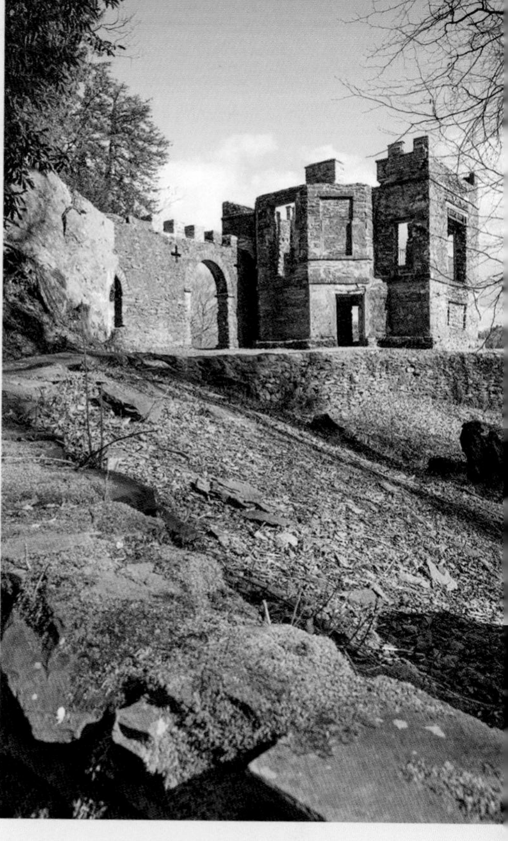

Claife Viewing Station looks out onto Windermere, which provided inspiration for Arthur Ransome's stories.

SOUTH EAST

Bateman's

Bateman's Lane, Burwash,
East Sussex TN19 7DS

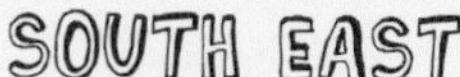

Filled with intriguing items from his travels in the East, Bateman's is very much as Rudyard Kipling left it. Nestled in the woodland of the Sussex Weald, it's an exciting place to visit for children of any age. There are always family-friendly activities to take part in, including a Jungle Book trail, Just So Stories days and tree climbing days.

Left: The garden at Hill Top, Cumbria.

17 Go glamping!

GREAT FOR

WEEKENDS • NATURE

Recent years have seen a surge in the popularity of camping holidays. It's a fantastic way to get the whole family outdoors and to simplify life, away from the pressures and distractions of the modern technological world. It's worth bearing in mind, however, that camping, especially in Britain, can have its downsides. If the rain falls on your carefully planned holiday week it can quickly turn from an activity-packed, fun-filled family dream into a complete nightmare. Snapped tent poles, leaky canvas, muddy fields and cold, miserable campers are not a recipe for fun and – if it's your first time in a tent – can be enough to put everyone off for life. And that's where glamping's so brilliant: it combines the away from it all feeling of camping with a weatherproof building and, often, heating, lighting and cooking. Far from being a soft option, we have found that when the weather isn't good it's possible to have a much greater range of adventures when you know there's a roaring fire and indoor kitchen to come back to.

Glamping comes in all shapes and sizes and there's an amazing variety of interesting and imaginative takes on the theme. We've seen everything from the traditional log cabins to buses and treehouses.

The National Trust has a great selection of glamping options, set in

Staying in one of the Long Valley yurts.

Low Wray, with Windermere in the background.

glorious surroundings with some of Britain's most spectacular landscapes on your doorstep. There's a yurt at Low Wray, right on the edge of Windermere, where ducks join you for breakfast and the rugged mountains tower beyond the gleaming water. Or a weekend at Clumber Park in a cosy pod, exploring the surrounding estate and the wider Sherwood Forest all around. Or perhaps a tipi at Great Langdale, snuggled into the glacial valley with the Langdale Pikes rising all around. There's much to choose from and each one is carefully positioned so you feel away from it all, in the wilds of the place, yet great facilities and hot croissants are only a short walk away. There are also many activities to choose from near to many of the Trust's campsites, from rock climbing and gorge scrambling to bushcraft and foraging.

We spent a week in a cosy Long Valley yurt at the National Trust's Low Wray campsite in Cumbria. As the snow fell around us we snuggled inside with a cosy log fire to keep us warm and a full kitchen to prepare our evening meals. We spent our days exploring the valleys between snow-covered mountains, knowing we had a warm and dry place to return to.

TOP TIPS

- Glamping comes in all shapes and sizes, from shepherds' huts to helicopters! Find a type that will capture your kids' imaginations.
- Glamping is a great way to sleep wild in winter, or when the British summer isn't as good as you'd hoped. Many come furnished with log burners, kitchens and comfy beds, so they're also a great way to introduce hesitant campers to the joys of outdoor living or add a touch of comfort and luxury to your camping trip.

Where to go

EAST MIDLANDS

Clumber Park Campsite

Worksop, Nottinghamshire S80 3AZ

At Clumber Park you can pitch your own tent or stay in a pod, wigwam or – if there are more of you – in the bunkhouse. The camping is in a pretty, peaceful setting bordered by trees. It's well away from the main visitor areas but also within an easy walk of the adventures that await you within the estate.

Camping pods at Clumber Park, Nottinghamshire.

NORTH WEST

Low Wray Campsite

Low Wray, Ambleside, Cumbria LA22 0JA

Situated on the quiet western shores of Windermere, glamping here comes in the form of pods, safari tents or yurts. There's a choice of locations from right at the water's edge to deep within the leafy woodland. The onsite shop is well stocked, there's an excellent playground and boat hire is available. Wray Castle is a gentle, scenic walk along the edge of the lake – a great day out exploring a castle with lots for kids to do.

NORTHERN IRELAND

Castle Ward Campsite

Downpatrick, County Down BT30 7LS

Turn a family day out into a glamping adventure at Castle Ward. There are comfortable pods and a bunkhouse for larger groups. This unique, eighteenth-century mansion stands on the shores of Strangford Lough, perfectly situated for walking, cycling, kayaking and many more family adventures.

Camping pods at Low Wray, Cumbria.

THE NEXT STEP: BIGGER CHALLENGES FOR UP AND COMING ADVENTURERS

This chapter's all about getting out and getting involved, from making your own adventure scrapbook to building a raft and sailing it. Climb trees and towers, explore caves and castles, or get curious about creatures. You might even find yourself on the set of your favourite film...

18 Explore a castle

There's something about a semi-ruined castle that seems to connect with kids on a deep level. Perhaps it's the maze of tunnels and the excitement of peering out through a slit window, or the spiral staircases leading up to airy towers, or the strange yet joyful feeling of being both indoors and outdoors at the same time. They're often in incredible places too. Twice a day, Holy Island – home to Lindisfarne Castle – becomes inaccessible as the causeway disappears below the tide, but it's a fine place to be stranded for a while, watching fulmars soar above the stormy North Sea from the tower.

The dramatic ruins of Corfe Castle have stood, proudly guarding the principal route through the Purbeck Hills, for a thousand years. It's a brilliant place to immerse yourself in the past, imagining the battles and sieges that took place before it was finally demolished in the seventeenth century during the English Civil War between the Cavaliers and the Roundheads. What an exciting way to learn history! There's even a self-guided Castle Quest booklet, available every day, filled with things to do including quiz questions, brass rubbings, puzzles and join-the-dots … with a prize at the end.

FASCINATING FACTS

- The National Trust looks after 17 castles across England and Wales, from ancient ruins to modern-day mansions.
- In total there are over 1,500 castle sites in England alone, although in some places very little remains visible.
- Castle Drogo, in Devon, was the last castle built in England and was completed in 1930, 19 years after construction began.
- The first castles in England appeared during the eleventh century.

Admiring Bodiam Castle, East Sussex.

Climbing one of the towers in Bodiam Castle, East Sussex.

The approach to the moated structure of Bodiam Castle, East Sussex, is awe-inspiring; from across the estate the medieval crenellated towers appear to rise straight from the water. Crossing the narrow walkway to the entrance, guarded by the original portcullis, you will see huge carp patrolling the dark water, gaping up at passers-by in the hope of some stray duck food. It's a great place for interactive learning too: dress up as a knight for St George's Day or have a go at archery in the grounds. There's some fascinating wildlife to discover, from the bats that hang in the towers to the wild bees and rare 'jet black' ants that live in one of the oak trees. But, in our opinion, simply exploring the incredible part-ruined insides of the castle is the most exciting thing to do at Bodiam. Jump through holes in the walls, scramble over, under and up the ruins, disappear into secret rooms and imagine what life would have been like for the castle's inhabitants hundreds of years ago. Make sure you climb the narrow spiral staircase that winds its way up one of the towers – an effort that's rewarded with great views from the top.

GREAT FOR **HISTORY • YOUNGER KIDS**

TOP TIPS

- Castles are exciting, but even getting to some can be an adventure! Take a boat across Lake Windermere to Wray Castle in Cumbria or catch a steam train to Bodiam and Corfe castles.
- Many National Trust castles are perfect places to learn about the country's history in a fun, interactive way, with dressing up, re-enactments and quests to take part in.

Where to go

SOUTH WEST

Corfe Castle

The Square, Wareham, Dorset BH20 5EZ

(not National Trust)

Corfe Castle is a survivor of the English Civil War, partially demolished in 1646 by the Parliamentarians. It's a great place to appreciate what 1,000 years of history feels like, and children and adults alike are captivated by these haunting ruins – and the breath-taking views out across the Purbeck countryside to the sea. There's a campsite next to the castle (not National Trust) if, like us, you don't want the adventure to end.

SOUTH EAST

Bodiam Castle

Bodiam, near Robertsbridge, East Sussex TN32 5UA

(Facilities are at the car park, a ten-minute walk from the castle. No facilities at the castle)

Fourteenth-century Bodiam Castle is everything a child needs a castle to be: massive, turreted, moated and with the original wooden portcullis. Walking over the moat towards the huge front entrance, carp gazing up at you from the murky waters, it feels like you've been transported back a few hundred years. Inside it's semi-ruined and exciting for kids to run around exploring. Head up the spiral staircase, passing slit windows for firing arrows at your enemies, and take in the glorious views from the top.

Left: Majestic Corfe Castle, Dorset.

Right: Family fun at Wray Castle, Cumbria.

NORTH WEST

Wray Castle

Low Wray, Ambleside, Cumbria LA22 0JA

Mock-Gothic Wray Castle looks more fun than foreboding, standing overlooking the lake at Windermere. Unlike many properties the interior is quite empty: perfect for kids to run around in without the worry of knocking over a priceless vase! This is a great place to stay in on a rainy day as there's plenty to do inside, including dressing up, a Peter Rabbit trail and an indoor play area.

19 Help out on the farm

Seeing a working farm in action is interesting and exciting for kids, as well as an essential part of understanding where the food they eat comes from. Watching cows being milked, sheep being sheared, squealing litters of piglets, and crops being grown and harvested helps them to grasp the whole cycle of production that's so absent from the neatly pre-packaged goods that sit on supermarket shelves.

There are lots of National Trust farms across the country, each with its own delights and activities to get involved in. As well as more traditional farms, many properties simply grow much of their own produce for use in their onsite cafés and restaurants. Walking around these kitchen gardens is always fascinating – and an inspiration for any mini gardeners who want to try growing some of their own food at home.

Home Farm, on the Wimpole Estate in the depths of the Cambridgeshire countryside, is buzzing with interesting things to see and do. As a rare breed farm it works hard to conserve rare and traditional breeds of livestock, including White Park cattle, Tamworth pigs, Bagot goats and four-horned Manx Loaghtan sheep. Children of all ages can get involved with taking care of the animals here: lambing time is especially busy with around 600 lambs expected each year (NB. pregnant women should avoid contact with lambing ewes). After all that hard work why not take a relaxing ride on a shire horse-drawn carriage or drive your own mini tractor? There's a well-stocked farm shop too so you can pick up a picnic of locally produced food.

Llanerchaeron in Ceredigion is a self-sufficient farm that is home to 11 different species of farm animals, all traditional breeds including Welsh Black cattle, Llanwenog sheep and Welsh pigs. Throughout the year visitors can get involved in helping out with everything from shearing to crop harvesting, as well as having the opportunity for contact with the animals.

Nestled in the orchards of County Armagh, Ardress House offers an insight into how farms worked centuries ago. With its eighteenth-century cobbled courtyard complete with tools from the time, it's easy to imagine how it must have been. Nowadays there's a friendly flock of chickens, some Shetland ponies and an incredible eight different species of bat.

FUN FACT

- Shire horses weigh a tonne each!

Getting involved on the farm – brushing a llama.

GREAT FOR
• NATURE • LEARNING

Where to go

EAST OF ENGLAND

Home Farm

Wimpole Estate, Arrington, Royston, Cambridgeshire SG8 0BW

(parkland only)

Home Farm is one of the country's largest rare breed centres set amidst a farmyard made up of eighteenth-century and modern buildings, with Shire horses, Longhorn and White Park cattle, pigs and sheep. It's a perfect place to get some hands-on experience of farming: grooming the donkeys, feeding the pigs or milking a cow! The wider Wimpole Estate is also a delight to visit, with vast areas of garden and parkland to explore.

WALES

Llanerchaeron

Ciliau Aeron, near Aberaeron, Ceredigion SA48 8DG

A remarkable, self-sufficient estate where families can learn all about growing food and farming. Visit the busy kitchen garden or head to the pole barn to get a close-up experience of lambing on a working farm. You can also help feed the lambs every day during the Easter holidays at 12pm and 4pm.

NORTH EAST

Gibside

near Rowlands Gill, Gateshead, Tyne & Wear NE16 6BG

Set within 600 acres of glorious Georgian estate, Gibside has lovely views of the Derwent Valley and miles of winding trails to explore. Make it a weekend adventure with a stay in a West Wood yurt and a wood-fired pizza from the Gibside pub.

20 Make a raft and sail it

Making a raft is a great activity to do with children, and their level of involvement will vary depending on their age. Younger children love helping to find and collect sticks of just the right size, and as they get older and their manual dexterity improves they'll be able to help tie the string and decorate the sails. It's a lot of fun to head to the pond, lake or river to set your rafts afloat – even the bath will do! Raft-building works well as a group activity too: split into teams and build a raft each, then race them against each other, or see whose will carry the most weight before it sinks.

Stick rafts can either be built entirely using natural materials that can be foraged in any woodland or, to make a more robust, longer lasting version you can lash them with string. Sails made from large, deciduous leaves such as sycamore or horse-chestnut are great in the summer months, but over winter, or for extra creativity, it works well to cut sails from squares of stiff cloth and decorate them using potato prints or fabric pens.

Rafts are scalable too, so older children can use bigger logs tied together with rope to make them large enough to sit on. A second – or even third – layer of logs works well to keep occupants clear of the water, and a pole for punting works better than a sail. It's a great way to get inventiveness flowing and rafts can be customised endlessly – for example you can add extra floatation in the form of barrels or even create a simple shelter on board.

Raft sailing on Dartmoor, Devon.

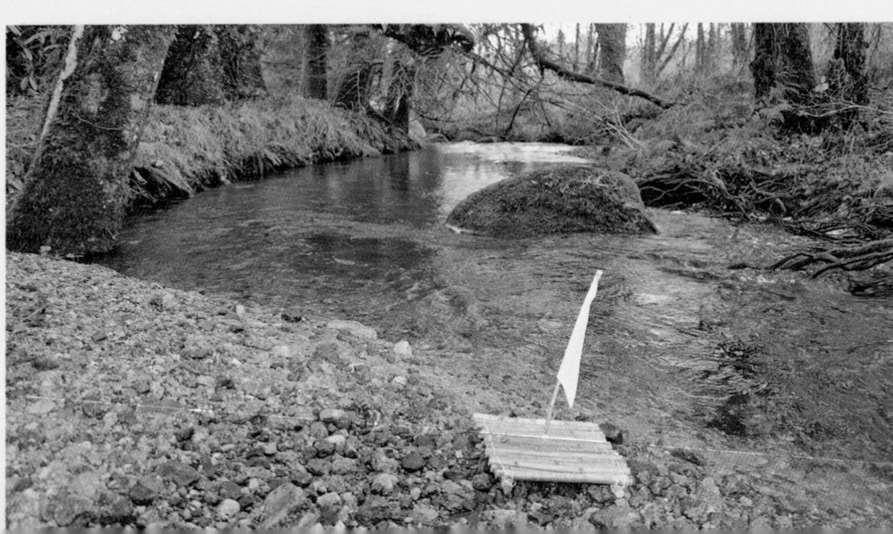

HOW TO BUILD YOUR RAFT

YOU WILL NEED

- 4 sticks of equal length to construct a frame
- around 10–15 sticks of the same length as those for the frame to create the bed of the raft
- 1 thinner stick for the mast
- 1 long grass reed/ stem or string for lashing sticks together
- 1 large leaf or triangle of paper/ card/fabric for the sail

1 Start by making the frame. Lay the four sticks out to create a square, with the ends slightly overlapping.

2 Secure the ends together by winding a reed or string around each join, creating a criss-cross and tying or tucking in the loose ends. Repeat for all four corners.

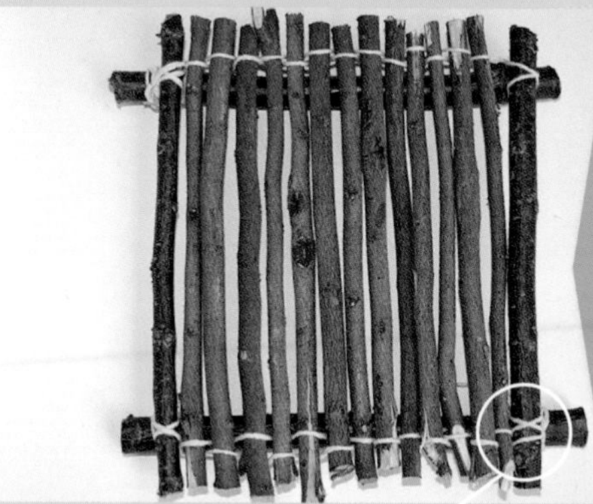

TIP! For larger rafts a second layer of sticks/logs can be added so that the top of the raft remains above the water even when loaded.

3 Once the frame is completed, **lie the remaining sticks parallel to each other** across the frame to create a raft 'bed'.

4 Secure them to the frame by weaving reed or string in and out of the sticks at both ends.

5 Once this is done you can also **lash the bed to the frame** in a couple of places for added robustness.

6 Take the leaf and make two small holes in it. Push the mast through the holes to **create a sail**. If using paper, card or fabric, you could also fold the triangle in half and glue it around the mast.

7 Insert your mast into a gap in between two of the sticks and secure it in place by tying with reed or string.

8 THE RAFT IS READY FOR SAILING!

20 Make a raft and sail it

Where to go

NORTH WEST

River Esk

Boot, Eskdale, Cumbria CA19 ITG

Mountains, tarns, the Ravenglass steam railway and the babbling Esk make this a perfect place for an adventure. Follow the Eskdale Trail from St Catherine's Church and you'll find shallows perfect for rafting and paddling; stepping stones to jump between and shady riverbanks where you can enjoy your picnic.

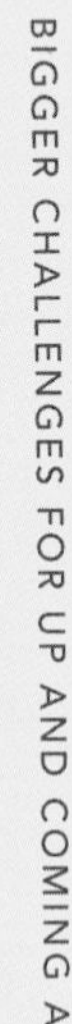

SOUTH WEST

Cotehele

St Dominick, near Saltash, Cornwall PL12 6TA

(estate only)

(at quay and main house)

There's a whole host of places to sail your raft at Cotehele, from ponds to the Morden stream that runs through the wooded valley to the still-working mill where you can see grain being ground into flour and made into biscuits and cakes ready for sampling. You can jump on a real boat to explore the River Tamar too.

Left: Sailing a full size raft at Brancaster, Norfolk.
Right: There are many opportunities to sail a model raft at Bodnant Garden, Conwy.

WALES

Bodnant Garden

Tal-y-Cafn, near Colwyn Bay, Conwy LL28 5RE

(selected days only)

Bodnant Garden is something special: a glorious display of colour, texture and perfume. Throughout the garden run watery features, perfect for setting sail a small raft. There's also an adventure trail and waymarked walk.

21 Complete a Parkrun

Families that run together have fun together! And there's no better way to have a weekly family running adventure than to go along to your local Parkrun.

Parkrun organises free, weekly, 5km timed runs around the world. They are open to everyone, are free, safe and easy to take part in. They've been going since 2004 and are now a global phenomenon with over two million registered runners and volunteers. Each Parkrun is organised by members of the local community with support from the national team; there's always a great atmosphere and getting involved in volunteering can be even more fun than the run itself. They are always friendly, sociable events and where there's a café onsite many runners will meet for a coffee and a chat afterwards.

FUN FACTS

- Parkrun was founded in 2004 in Bushy Park, London. It's now a global success: in 2016 more than 100,000 people took part in over 850 events, plus 92 junior Parkruns.
- There are over two million registered Parkrunners globally.
- Each Parkrun event is organised entirely by volunteers.

Some venues hold a junior Parkrun for ages 4 to 14 too: 2k events that children can run on their own or with an adult. It's a brilliantly low-pressure way to introduce youngsters to the enjoyment and challenge of running, and the satisfaction of completing a distance.

Parkruns happen every weekend in pleasant open spaces with a course suitable for runners of all abilities. You can even run with a buggy. Many National Trust places make wonderful Parkrun venues so you can take in the splendour of an estate, meet friends, get some enjoyable exercise in the great outdoors and then follow it all up with a day out.

You don't need to go to an official event to have fun running together as a family of course. If you don't feel you're ready to go the full distance yet, why not try a race around the garden or a run at

Lining up at the start of a Junior Parkrun.

your local park, or start by completing a kilometre and then gradually build up? Running is fun, free and a great way to stay fit, whatever your age – and a great lifelong habit to get kids into too.

GREAT FOR

• ACTIVE

TOP TIPS

- Parkrun is fun, free and for everyone – the whole family can run together.
- Go to parkrun.org.uk to register and print out a barcode before your first Parkrun.
- Once you have your barcode, simply turn up at the start – and have fun!

Where to go

Bath Skyline, Somerset
Belton House, Lincolnshire
Blickling Estate, Norfolk
Castle Coole, County Fermanagh
Clumber Park, Nottinghamshire
Colby Woodland Garden, Pembrokeshire
Fell Foot, Cumbria
Fountains Abbey, North Yorkshire
Gibside, Tyne & Wear
Hatfield Forest, Essex
Killerton, Devon
Lanhydrock, Cornwall
Lyme, Cheshire
Montacute House, Somerset
Nostell, West Yorkshire
Osterley Park, London
Parke, Dartmoor, Devon
Penrhyn Castle, Gwynedd
Penrose, Cornwall
Plymbridge Woods, Devon
Sheringham Park, Norfolk
The Leas, Tyne & Wear
Tredegar House, Monmouthshire
Wimpole, Cambridgeshire (also Junior Parkrun)

22 Explore a cave

Even finding the caves at Cathedral Quarries in the heart of the Lake District feels like an adventure. The way there is unmarked, and when you arrive there are signs leaving you in no doubt that any risks you take are your own. But venture onwards a little further to discover the magic... This is an incredible place: from the dark tunnels at the start it opens up into an airy cavern where shards of clear light enter through interesting rock formations. It's a great place to go rock climbing too, and there's often some entertainment to be found in watching the climbers scale the sheer faces and abseil back down again – great viewing for any budding mountaineers. You'll need wellies as it's often wet underfoot and a torch for the tunnels.

For younger children there's some great exploring to be done in the small caves at Stourhead in Wiltshire – they're straightforward to scramble up to and sit inside, watching the world go by. You could even tick off a couple of other

Looking out from the caves at St Anthony Head in Cornwall.

adventures here, such as heading off for a walk or bike ride around the lake or climbing one of the statuesque trees.

A full 100 steps lead down to Lydstep Caverns in Pembrokeshire. These arched, limestone caves have been hollowed out by the sea, and are only accessible at low tide, so a visit needs to be carefully timed but is well worth it. With sandy floors and plenty of scattered boulders they make for exciting exploring. The views out to sea are beautiful too: huge flocks of seabirds; the islands of Caldey and Lundy, whose lighthouses beam out into the darkness at night; and even dolphins and porpoises if you're lucky. There's a gentle, family-friendly mile-long walk around the headland, passing relics of the Second World War (an intriguing introduction to contemporary history) and glorious coastal views.

FUN FACTS

- The sport of exploring caves is known as 'spelunking'.
- Titan (not National Trust) is a natural cavern near Castleton in the Derbyshire Peak District, and is the deepest shaft of any known cave in Britain, at 141.5m (464ft); that's one-and-a-half times the height of Big Ben!
- Creswell Crags (not National Trust), also in Derbyshire, contains Ice Age rock art, tools and engravings.

TOP TIPS

- Caves are brilliant to explore but can be a bit dark and damp. Take a head torch and wellies with you.

GREAT FOR

LEARNING • NATURE • ACTIVE

Where to go

NORTH WEST

Cathedral Cavern Quarries

Little Langdale, Coniston, Cumbria

These vast, open caves are exhilarating to explore, with shafts of light falling through great openings and platforms to clamber on. The long, dark adit tunnel (a horizontal tunnel used to access a mine) is particularly exciting, but you'll need a torch. The caves are a 25-minute walk from Little Langdale.

WALES

Lydstep Caverns

Lydstep, Tenby, Pembrokeshire SA70 7SE

An enjoyable and family-friendly 1-mile (1.6km) walk takes you from the car park around above the cliffs, with uninterrupted views out across to Lundy Island on a clear day. The 100 steps (on the right just after the car park) that lead down to the caverns are fine for confident walkers and the caves are well worth the expedition. NB: the caverns are only accessible at low tide so check the times if you want to explore them.

View across the cliffs at Lydstep Headland, Pembrokeshire.

MIDLANDS

Holy Austin Rock Houses

Compton Road, Kinver, near Stourbridge, Staffordshire DY7 6DL

(not National Trust)

The Holy Austin Rock Houses at Kinver Edge aren't like any ordinary caves. They've been cosily restored with chairs and a stove; make yourselves comfortable and let the volunteers tell you all about their history. Once you've finished exploring, head out onto Kinver Edge: a wild and windswept heathland where you'll find wildlife, woodland and the ramparts of an imposing Iron Age hill fort.

Kinver Edge and the Rock Houses, Staffordshire.

23 Make a home for a creature

Solitary bee house

Bees are important pollinators – essential for over 250,000 species of plant worldwide. Solitary bees are so called because they don't live in colonies like honey bees. There are over 200 different species of solitary bee in Britain, some of which look quite different from the bees we're used to seeing. One species, *Ceratina cyanea*, is small and metallic blue. These bees have diverse nesting habits, so making them a home that they can customise as they wish is a great idea, and very straightforward too.

How to do it:

Bundle together several hollow bamboo canes and tie them with string. Hang in a sheltered, dry spot and watch carefully for bees to arrive.

Bug hotel

You can see bug hotels in action at many National Trust properties; they're easy to build, can be made entirely out of recycled materials and are a perfect addition to any garden or outdoor space.

Homemade bug hotel using an old bird box.

A British garden may contain up to 2,000 different species of insect so there will always be something new to look at.

How to do it:

Some insects like damp, shady places whereas others prefer sun, so choose a flat, solid surface that's partly shaded. Wooden pallets make a perfect base for your bug hotel, and you can make it as large as you like by adding more pallets on top. Fill each gap with something different to mimic the sort of environments bugs love: dead wood for beetles; bamboo canes for bees; dry

Right: A luxury bug hotel made using pallets.

leaves and sticks; rocks; hay and straw. You could even grow some wild flowers on your hotel to encourage pollinators.

Hedgehog house

Hedgehogs are wonderful garden visitors, eating the slugs that would otherwise steal our lettuces, and they're fun, rewarding night-time creatures for kids to spot. However their numbers have declined by 30% over the last decade due to loss of habitat. You can help by making a hedgehog house.

How to do it:

Making a hedgehog house is easy: simply take a sturdy crate or wooden box (an old wine box works well) and make a hole at least 17cm (7in) wide in one end to allow hedgehogs to come and go. Drill a couple of extra holes in the sides for ventilation. Place the box upside down in a quiet, shaded part of the garden that won't be disturbed and cover with sticks, grass and leaves. Leave the hole open – or even better, add on a short tunnel leading to the entrance.

TOP TIPS

- Making a home for a creature is a great activity that all the family can get involved in. Structures like bug hotels are fascinating to watch, a great source of learning and a brilliant way to provide safe habitat for our essential wild things.

GREAT FOR YOUNGER KIDS • NATURE

24 Create an adventure journal

A journal or scrapbook is ideal for recording a family adventure, from a weekend away to a full year in your local park or woods. It's a great way to get creative and make a lasting record of a place or adventure – and a fun project for the whole family to get involved in. You can take the journal with you and build it as you go or make it once you get home with everything you've collected on your trip. A journal can be a collection of anything you want to put in it – the end result should sum up the whole experience and be a thing to treasure. Make it bright and colourful and include plenty of notes to help you re-live the trip once it's over. Here are some of our favourite things to include:

Stories

Get kids to talk or write about some of their favourite experiences of the trip – encourage them to recall details such as sights, sounds, smells and tastes. Get them to be descriptive, for example

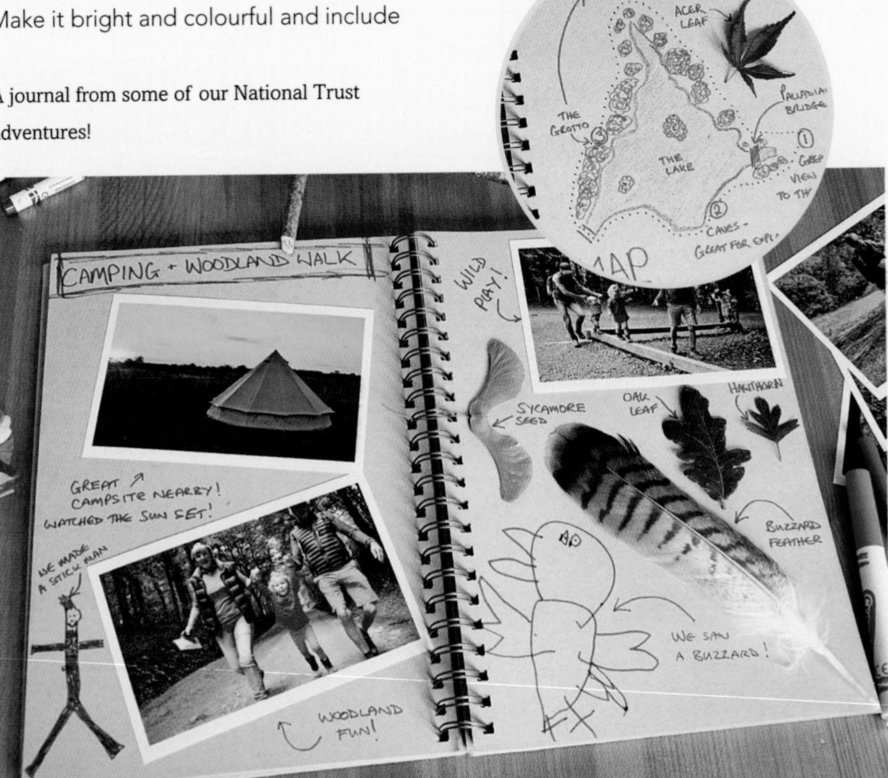

A journal from some of our National Trust adventures!

GREAT FOR

CREATIVE
• NATURE • LEARNING

TOP TIPS

- Let kids pick the book they want to use as a journal, or help them make their own. Make it fun and personalise it by designing a new cover that reflects the adventure. And remember to collect as you go!

explaining how it feels to swim in the sea; walk on the beach; have the wind blowing in their hair; or the warm sun shining on their faces.

Photographs

Include as many photos of your family's adventures as you can – and let the kids take their own pictures too. Remember, bad weather is no reason not to take the camera – it's when some of the best photos can be snapped.

Tickets

Train tickets, steam-train tickets, tickets for boat rides or theatre trips; collect them all and stick them in!

Poems

Writing poetry is a great way to encourage children to think differently about an experience. Rather than simply telling a story about what happened they need to think about how it made them feel. Making up fun rhymes and limericks is good for getting everyone involved and laughing too.

Drawings

Younger kids love telling stories through drawings, so get them creating scenes they can then stick things onto. Older children could illustrate the book with designs or use it as a sketch book to record some of the things they see.

Leaves and flowers

Collecting a few interesting things along the way, such as leaves, flowers, seeds, acorns and small shells is great for adding texture and 3D to your book. Flowers and leaves can be pressed before you use them – this removes any moisture from them and keeps their colour. Simply lie them flat between two sheets of absorbent paper and pop them into a heavy book. Another couple of books on top of that one are a good idea too. After about four weeks they'll be pressed and ready to use.

25 Go tree climbing

Tree climbing is one of our favourite family activities. It's absorbing, entertaining, fun and rewarding and many National Trust places, with their abundant woodland and mature deciduous trees, make perfect venues.

First there's the challenge of finding the perfect climbing tree. It must have branches low enough to reach – although small children are surprisingly adept at climbing up to these. Branches should be strong and healthy and evenly spaced, and ideally there should be some resting points created by dividing branches where you can stop and admire your leafy world, or watch those at ground level go by, oblivious of you hidden away in your lofty position. Teach children to look for good branches that will take their weight – and how to spot dead branches that won't. And be prepared to climb up and get them – like cats, kids are often better at climbing up than getting down again!

Enjoying the view from a higher perspective at Dunham Massey, Cheshire.

There's a wonderful variety to be found in trees: the textures of the leaves and bark, from the smooth beech to the knobbly pear; the range of techniques required to make an ascent; the different smells from woody pine to fruity apple; and the sounds each tree makes as the wind moves through it. Each tree feels different too: there are the sturdy branches of an oak that you can get your whole arm around, the complex puzzle of old rhododendrons, the ladder-like conifers and the delicate willow.

If you fancy exploring the treetops but prefer to do so under the tutelage of an expert and with ropes, harnesses and a zip wire or a rope swing to play on, there are organised tree climbing events at some National Trust properties throughout the summer months. These are a lot of fun and very popular, so it's

Climbing the huge branches of the monumental Japanese Cedar at Trelissick in Cornwall.

worth booking in advance. Fell Foot Park in Cumbria is great for organised tree-climbing races!

A good climbing tree local to your home (in your garden if you're lucky) is a great thing for any child to have. It gives them a refuge, a hideout, a climbing frame and a place to explore and experience nature right up close. Climbing is a great skill to master, requiring strength, agility and body-awareness that will build confidence and help with other sports. And sitting high up in the branches is a great way to experience a different perspective too, whatever age you are.

TOP TIPS

- If you haven't climbed a tree for a while, or your children are new to it, take it slowly and start with lower branches to get used to the experience – especially the feeling of being high up.
- Look for trees with plenty of branches low down to make starting your climb easier.
- Make sure any branch you put your weight on is strong and healthy – look for leaves and new shoots growing off it. Dead branches will have no new growth and are likely to snap under your weight.
- Remember, you need to be able to climb back down again – often much more tricky than climbing up!

GREAT FOR

ACTIVE • NATURE

Where to go

SOUTH WEST

Woodchester Park

Nympsfield, near Stonehouse, Gloucestershire GL10 3TS

(not National Trust, only when mansion open)

Entering the secret, wooded valley of Woodchester Park is like visiting another time. It's peaceful, enchanting, exciting and relaxing – all at once. The woodland play trail makes it perfect for families and there are mature trees everywhere just waiting to be climbed. In the centre of the valley there's a lake with carp in it and an unfinished mansion (not National Trust).

Conifer climbing.

EAST MIDLANDS

Belton House

Grantham, Lincolnshire NG32 2LS

(dogs in selected areas)

Belton House is a fantastic place to take kids. The woodland is filled with perfect climbing trees; there are swathes of lawn and parkland to play on; there's the biggest and best outdoor play area we've found anywhere (almost as much fun for adults as for kids); rides on a miniature train; an indoor soft play area; and a wildlife area. There are cafés in both play areas too, so you can take a break from family adventuring for a few moments and let the kids amuse themselves.

NORTH WEST

Speke Hall

The Walk, Speke, Liverpool L24 1XD

A rare timber-framed Tudor manor house on the banks of the River Mersey, Speke Hall is a wonderful place to escape to. Surrounded by peaceful grounds and woodland it's fun for all sorts of adventures, but tree climbing's a real delight here. The collar of woodland that surrounds the estate is filled with interesting trees of different shapes and sizes – perfect for some leafy exploration.

Climbing through the puzzle of rhododendron branches at Longshaw Estate in Derbyshire.

26 Explore a film set

Unsurprisingly, given the wide range of beautiful houses, sweeping parkland and dramatic landscapes the National Trust looks after, many of its places star as locations for film and television productions. It's an exciting feeling, wandering around a place that's familiar from a favourite film, imagining the action happening, perhaps even a spot of re-enactment... These places were chosen for their atmosphere and presence, so they naturally make great places to visit.

Lavenham Guildhall features in the Harry Potter films as the derelict Potter house.

The adventures of J. K. Rowling's young wizard, Harry Potter, connect with people across nations and generations. The series of films was shot in a range of spectacular locations, including several National Trust properties and landscapes. Some of the cloisters scenes and Professor Snape's potions classes were shot at Lacock Abbey in Wiltshire.

A visit to Lacock Abbey and village makes for an enjoyable and varied day out for families of any age. The thirteenth-century village has been used in many productions including *Pride and Prejudice*, *Moll Flanders* and *Emma*, as well as for Godric's Hollow in *Harry Potter*. Almost all of the village is owned by the National Trust and is perfectly preserved; stepping into it really feels like travelling back in time. The Abbey itself is a beautiful Bath stone country house with monastic history. It's set in glorious 'Capability' Brown landscape that's ripe for exploration, with a ha-ha ditch for hiding and stunning wildflower meadows for spotting butterflies. There's a hand-powered carousel that – in bright sunshine – casts rainbows all around, and usually an adventure trail for kids to take part in. Exciting, winding trails, lined with wild garlic in spring, run through Victorian woodland – perfect for a walk with the buggy and plenty of great trees for climbing too. The Fox Talbot museum, housed within the Abbey, describes the development of modern photography by former resident William Henry Fox Talbot. It's a fascinating insight into the process and is presented in way that will interest children too. A great visit for projects on photography.

TOP TIPS

- Choose a place that's featured in a favourite film or series. Perhaps even follow up your visit by watching the film so the kids can spot where they've been

Many film locations, such as the Lavenham Guildhall in Suffolk shown in several scenes in *Harry Potter and the Deathly Hallows*, were filmed without the actors present. They were then transformed using CGI and the action – shot elsewhere – was superimposed.

The cloisters at Lacock Abbey, Wiltshire.

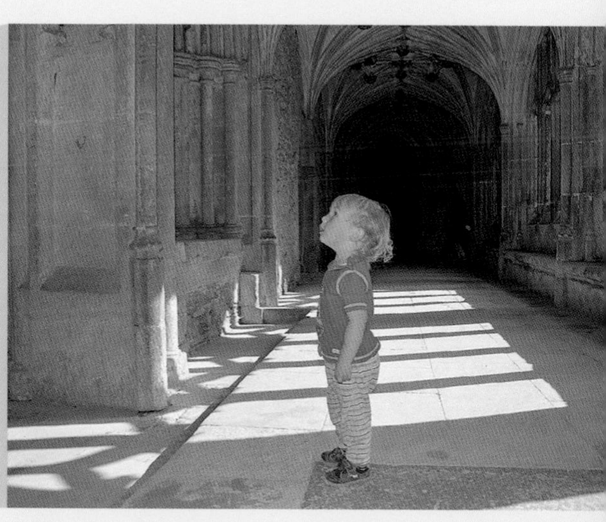

FUN FACT

- Hundreds of film and television productions have been shot at National Trust locations. See the 'Film and television' section of the Handbook for a full list. We've included a selection of the best for families on pages 122–123.

26
Explore a film set

Where to go

SOUTH WEST

Lacock Abbey and village

Lacock, near Chippenham, Wiltshire
SN15 2LG

(at certain times)

Lacock Abbey is steeped in history, housing nuns some 800 years ago. It's a fascinating place to wander around, and great for young children to explore and older children to recognise from the Harry Potter films. The Warming Room, with its 500-year-old cauldron, was used for Professor Snape's potions class. The characterful village – owned by the National Trust but with a community of residents – has also been featured in many television and film productions.

SOUTH EAST

Lavenham Guildhall

Market Place, Lavenham, Sudbury, Suffolk
CO10 9QZ

This beautiful and intriguing Tudor building stands at the heart of a picturesque and well-preserved village. There's plenty to do for families here, including dressing up and a children's trail. It was used as Harry's parents' derelict house in the first Harry Potter film.

The teacup-shaped topiary at Antony, Cornwall.

Exploring the grounds of Antony House, Cornwall.

Other places to go

SOUTH WEST

Antony

Torpoint, Cornwall PL11 2QA

The gardens at Antony are an adventure to explore in their own right. Complex, intricate, yet still fun and relaxed, there are hideaways everywhere for children to investigate. This atmospheric place shone as the setting for Tim Burton's blockbuster film *Alice in Wonderland*.

SOUTH EAST

Ashridge Estate

Moneybury Hill, Ringshall, Near Berkhamsted, Hertfordshire HP4 1LT

Disney filmed some of the scenes for *Maleficent* and *Into the Woods* among the densely wooded landscape of Ashridge. But that's just the start… There's so much exploring to be done on this 5,000-acre estate in the Chiltern Hills, perfect for cycling, walking and adventuring. Some walks are buggy-friendly; ask for details.

27 Go sledging

Sledging is fast, fun and a fantastic way to get out into the hills and play in the snow. With a little preparation it can be enjoyed in relative safety – just follow our top tips below:

TOP TIPS

1 Make sure you can steer and stop your sledge – bags and trays might seem like a good idea but they're very hard to control.

2 Sit up on your sledge with your legs in front of you. Going head first or standing up is much more likely to result in injury.

3 A properly fitted bike helmet will help prevent head injuries.

4 Choose a hill with a gentle slope and a long runoff area so the sledge can slow down and stop safely.

5 Start with a small hill to get used to controlling the sledge before working up to the bigger ones.

6 Make sure the hill is free of potential hazards such as trees and rocks.

7 Wait until the hill is free from other people before heading down.

8 Always be aware of other sledgers as well as walkers, dogs and anyone else using the hill.

One of the snowiest winters we've experienced in Britain happened when we were lucky enough to live within the Peak District National Park in Derbyshire. There was snow on the ground from early November until Easter; it drifted along the verges, creating fascinating, intricate, wind-blown sculptures. In places it filled up the lanes completely – as high as the hedges either side. We were able to walk over gates and jump into waist-deep snow. There were snowball fights, snow sculptures, snow caves and snow angels. And, of course, plenty of sledging. In a country where quantities of snow are fairly rare, it's always met with excitement, and the way it transforms the landscape and seems to bring everything else to a halt makes snowy days some of the best for family adventures.

Everyone has a local hill that's perfect for sledging. One of our favourite places that snowy winter in Derbyshire was Mam Tor, an iconic hill in the High Peak region. It's a popular place and there were often others sledging too – some even brought their skis! We started our sledging on the easier slopes and progressed to the steeper ones as we gained confidence.

Sledging is great for all ages and abilities, from those who like to go as fast as possible to smaller children who love to be pulled along. Try building a course

to navigate little children through, with twists, turns and some gentle slopes – they'll love to get involved in the excitement too.

GREAT FOR

ACTIVE • WINTER

Sledging at Box Hill, Surrey.

Where to go

SOUTH EAST

Dunstable Downs and Whipsnade Estate

Whipsnade Road, Dunstable, Bedfordshire LU6 2GY

The highest point in Bedfordshire, Dunstable Downs is a great place to go in winter to slide down the snow-covered chalk hillsides. The views from the top are breathtaking and there's a great variety of slopes to choose from. Also fantastic for a summer visit, when this SSSI (Site of Specific Scientific Interest) is buzzing with wildlife, and on a windy spring or autumn day to go kite flying.

WEST MIDLANDS

Downs Banks

Washdale Lane, Oulton Heath, Near Stone, Staffordshire ST15 8UU

Just a short trip from many of the Midlands' busiest places, Downs Banks is a haven of peace and tranquillity – and a great place to go sledging! Escape here to walk in the woods and watch the wildlife. During the warmer months the brook is great for paddling and the downs are excellent for flying kites.

Sledging in the Peak District, Derbyshire.

EAST MIDLANDS

Mam Tor

near Castleton, Derbyshire S33 8WA

Mam Tor is a perfect mini-mountain for aspiring climbers, with a straightforward walk from the car park to the summit where panoramic views await. In winter it's a popular spot for sledging, with lots of slopes of different gradients.

Making snowballs on Dartmoor, Devon.

28 Fly a kite

Getting your first kite and learning to fly it is a rite of passage for many children. It's exhilarating and hugely enjoyable once you've mastered the basics. As kids we regularly headed out to a local hill on a dry windy day, traipsed to the top and let fly our assortment of kites, often those we'd made from tissue paper and doweling. It's a tradition we're now enjoying passing on to our own kids – and it's still just as exciting!

There are many different kites available to buy – and it's fun to experiment and make your own too. Different types of kite fly best in different conditions. In general, diamond and delta kites fly best in light winds, hexagon kites in moderate winds and box kites in stronger winds. Always fly kites in wide, open spaces and be aware of what's around you at all times, including people, trees, cars, animals, horse riders, water, cliff edges and electricity cables. The Kite Society (www.thekitesociety.org.uk) has lots of useful information and guidance for those wanting to get into kite flying.

Here are our top tips for successful kite flying:

Choose your kite

Choose a kite to match the wind conditions and the person flying the kite. A big, powerful kite may well be too much to handle for a smaller child, whereas a teenager will probably love a kite that can do stunts and fly in stronger winds.

Choose your day

Choose a clear, dry day with a gentle breeze. If you're heading for a hill you'll

The Dunstable Kite Festival, Bedfordshire.

GREAT FOR • FESTIVALS • ACTIVE

find the wind often picks up the higher you go. Never fly kites in an electrical storm.

Have a go … and have fun!

Kite flying works best with one person holding the handle and line and another person holding the kite in the air with about 10m (33ft) of taught line between the two. The person flying the kite should have their back to the wind. When the person holding the kite lets go, gradually unravel the line to around 20m (66ft) as the kite rises into the air. Then it's a matter of pulling the line to make the kite go higher or releasing to make it drop.

The National Trust holds kite-flying festivals, which are a great way to get inspired about the world of kite flying. There are professional displays, family activities, local artists and plenty of entertainment for all – and of course a perfect opportunity to fly your own kite.

The biggest UK kite festival is probably Bristol's International Kite Festival (not National Trust), held in August each year on Durdham Down, a stunning green space close to the dramatic Avon Gorge on the northern edge of the city.

FUN FACTS

- It's thought kites were invented in China in the fifth century BC. Early kites were made from silk and bamboo.
- Kites are great fun to fly, but they've also been used for human flight, by the military, for science and meteorology, photography, generating power, aerodynamics experiments, and much more.

A marvellous boat-shaped kite.

28
Fly a kite

Where to go

SOUTH EAST

South Foreland Lighthouse

St Margaret's Bay, Dover, Kent CT15 5NA

South Foreland Lighthouse proudly guards the White Cliffs of Dover, and was the first lighthouse to use an electric light. Getting here is a mini adventure: there's no vehicular access so you'll need to park at one of the nearby National Trust car parks either a 1- or 2-mile (1.6 or 3.2km) walk away. Kite flying is a speciality here, with the breeze straight off the sea. You can even borrow a kite from the shop, which also sells ice-creams. From the top of the tower on a clear day you can see across the Channel to France.

The Dunstable Kite Festival in Bedfordshire.

NORTH WEST

Lyme

Disley, Stockport, Cheshire SK12 2NR

Nestling on the edge of the Peak District, Lyme's 1,300 acres are filled with things to explore, whether you're cycling, walking, picnicking in the sun or walking around the picturesque lake. The higher, wilder areas are perfect for kite flying – and there's an annual kite festival too. Down near the house there's a huge playground with options for younger and older children.

A kite-making workshop.

NORTHERN ISLAND

Downhill Demesne

Mussenden Road, Castlerock, County Londonderry BT51 4RP

Perched on a windswept headland, Downhill Demesne is a beautiful place to fly a kite, and there's a kite festival here each summer. You can also explore the remains of the grand house, destroyed by fire in 1851, take on the Bishop's Play Trail or feed the chickens at nearby Hezlett House.

KITE FESTIVALS

- Dunstable Downs, Bedfordshire
- Downhill Demesne, County Londonderry
- Berrington Hall, Herefordshire
- Lyme, Cheshire

29 Walk in a stream

There's nothing quite like cool water on bare feet. Paddling in the sea with the sand shifting beneath you; sitting by a river and dangling your toes in to catch the current; the pleasure of cold water after a long, hot walk – we relish them all. From the moment they are physically able, children love playing in water. It starts with the absolute glee of splashing in puddles and grows from there; a nearby and relatively safe watery place has to be one of the best locations for a day's adventuring. Paddle, skim stones, play pooh-sticks, make rope swings over the water, spot wildlife, set sail, forage… The list is endless.

We've always enjoyed going for walks along the edge of a stream, following the course of a river on one of many waterside trails across the country. But something of a recent discovery is the thrill of going for a walk actually in the stream; navigating it from within, feeling the stones under your feet and the current against your legs as you travel. It's a different perspective, seeing the world from stream's-eye-view, peering under the banks where the water has cut into the earth, stooping below trees that reach long branches down to the surface, feeling your way with each exploratory footstep. And all around is the sound of rushing, burbling water that's mesmerising and a perfect soundtrack for the exploration.

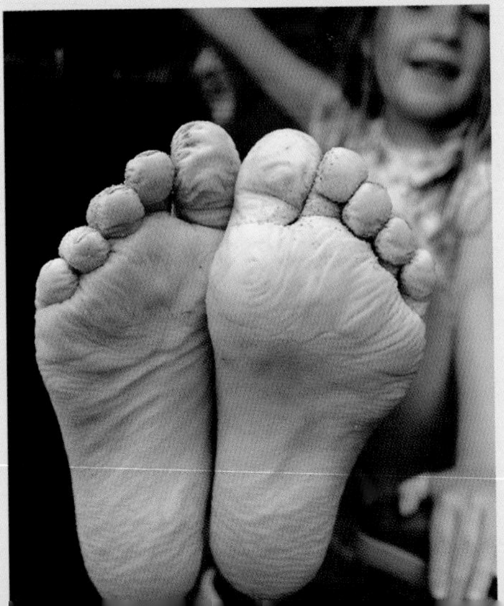

The best streams to walk in are those with plenty of shallow stretches, and some deep pools too. These can be quite strange to walk through as they stay cold, even on the warmest of days. Boulders are exciting to explore around, and their shadows may well conceal fish and other aquatic creatures.

Walking in a stream is a great topic to get kids to write or talk about, describing the feelings and the sounds they experience and the different things they encounter along the way.

Left: Prune feet!

Right: Paddling in the River Esk.

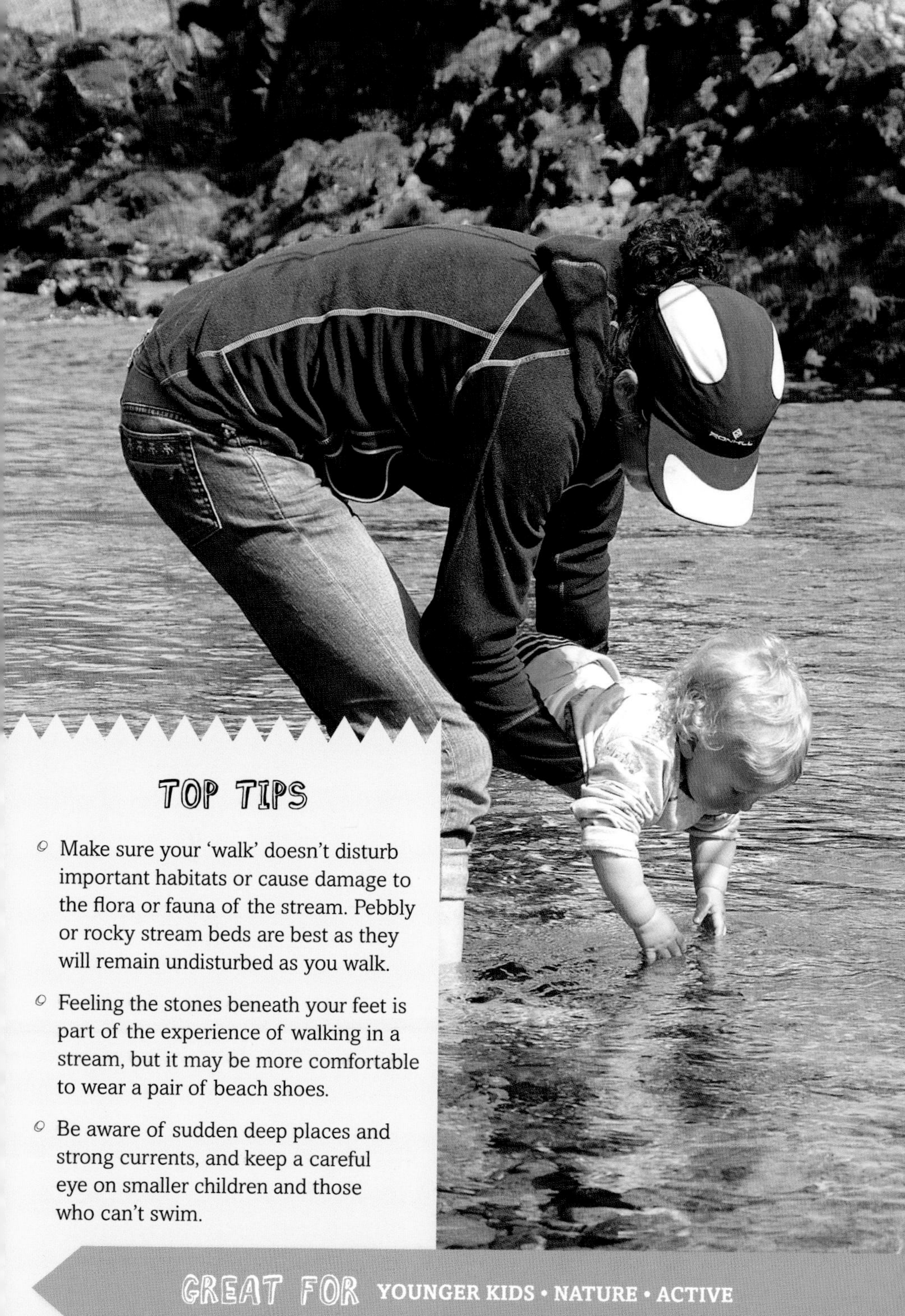

TOP TIPS

- Make sure your 'walk' doesn't disturb important habitats or cause damage to the flora or fauna of the stream. Pebbly or rocky stream beds are best as they will remain undisturbed as you walk.
- Feeling the stones beneath your feet is part of the experience of walking in a stream, but it may be more comfortable to wear a pair of beach shoes.
- Be aware of sudden deep places and strong currents, and keep a careful eye on smaller children and those who can't swim.

GREAT FOR YOUNGER KIDS • NATURE • ACTIVE

Where to go

WALES

Colby Woodland Garden

near Amroth, Pembrokeshire SA67 8PP

(in some areas)

There's much to discover in the hidden wooded valley at Colby. The shallow babbling stream that runs through its centre is perfect for playing. Walk along it, following it on a journey against the current, letting the path of the stream take you on its own adventure. It's perfect for paddling, sailing rafts or simply sitting with a picnic and enjoying the surroundings.

Playing in Burbage Brook on the Longshaw Estate, Derbyshire.

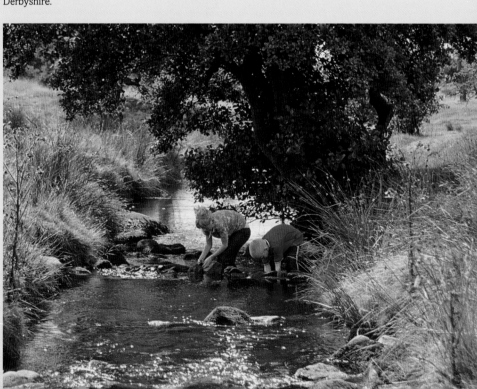

EAST MIDLANDS

Burbage Brook at Longshaw Estate

Longshaw, Derbyshire S11 7TZ

There's always something on for families at Longshaw: explore the boggart (a mischievous woodland creature) settlements, follow treasure trails, climb through rhododendrons or trace the waymarked trails to reach Burbage Brook, a perfect stream to walk along. The area around Padley Gorge can get busy at times, but walk a little way in either direction and you'll find plenty of paddling all to yourselves.

SOUTH WEST

Plymbridge Woods

Plymbridge Road, Plympton, Plymouth, Devon PL7 4SR

This is a popular, family-friendly part of Dartmoor, with events all year, a sensory trail and an orienteering course. The River Plym is shallow enough to walk in here, with some lovely deeper pools. It's a great place to see some of Dartmoor's wildlife too, with a peregrine viewing platform at Cann Viaduct during the spring months.

Balancing in the stream at Watersmeet, Exmoor, Devon.

30 Climb to the top of a tower

A little like climbing a mountain, climbing all the way to the top of a tall tower is a challenge that's rewarded by a sense of achievement – and often great views too. Most kids naturally love to climb and their enjoyment of being up high is often greater than that of their parents! Climbing a tower is such a simple adventure, but one that can also be an exploration of so many other things: history, architecture, geography, physics, even psychology…

The top of Leith Hill Tower in Surrey is the highest point in south-east England and a great tower for climbing. Count the 74 steps as you wind your way to the top where you're met with glorious panoramic views. With the help of the in-situ telescope you might be able to spot some of London's landmarks such as Wembley Stadium, the London Eye and Big Ben. And to the south lies the English Channel – how many boats can you spot?

Leith Hill is a great place for a family day out and once you're back on solid ground there's plenty to explore in the surrounding Surrey Hills countryside. It's very dog-friendly too. Stay until dusk to watch bats flitting through the air in search of insects or visit the bird hide in Rhododendron Wood. You could even make a weekend of it with a stay at the nearby National Trust Henman Bunkhouse.

There are some more unusual towers to climb too: the red-and-white-striped Greco-Gothic square tower at Gribbin Head in Cornwall was erected in 1832 to guide sailors away from the treacherous rocks of St Austell Bay and into the safety of the deep waters at Falmouth Harbour. The tower is open every Sunday from July to September, when you have the opportunity to climb all 109 steps to the top and admire the breathtaking Cornish coastal scenery.

Castles are great places to find towers to climb – a fun extra challenge to add

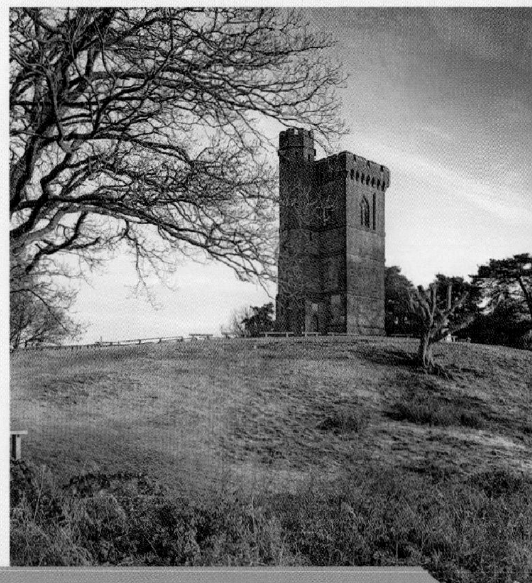

GREAT FOR LEARNING • YOUNGER CHILDREN • ACTIVE

to exploring a castle (page 94). The huge towers at Bodiam Castle, East Sussex, give you a taste of what it would have been like to defend this awe-inspiring place back in the fourteenth century – you can even dress up as a real live knight for the day. Scamper up the spiral staircase to the airy rooftop for fine views out across the Rother Valley.

Below: Descending the staircase at Souter Lighthouse, Tyne & Wear.

Bottom: Leith Hill Tower, Surrey.

Where to go

Bembridge Windmill, Isle of Wight
Alfred's Tower, Stourhead, Wiltshire
Leith Hill Tower, Surrey
Gribbin Head, Cornwall (Sundays, July – September)
Chirk Castle, Wrexham
Belvedere Tower, Surrey
Gatehouse Tower, Knole, Kent
Souter Lighthouse, Tyne & Wear
Hardy Monument, Dorset
Panorama Tower, Croome, Worcestershire (selected days only)
South Foreland Lighthouse, Kent
Bodiam Castle, East Sussex

FUN FACTS

- The top of Leith Hill Tower in Surrey is the highest point in the south of England at 329m (1,079ft) above sea-level.

31 Travel back in time

We know it's not really possible to travel back in time – although that would be an exciting adventure to write about! – but the science of archaeology helps us to understand what happened hundreds, and even thousands, of years ago. From standing stones and drawings in the hillside to the remains of ancient settlements, archaeology provides a fascinating window into the past. It's like a treasure hunt to find pieces and fit them together to create a picture – one that enables us to understand more about life in an entirely different time.

We arrived at the World Heritage Site of Avebury in Wiltshire shortly after sunrise. It was early summer and the standing stones cast long, dark shadows on the sunlit grass. Everything was bathed in golden light, from the high banks and ditches of the henge to the surrounding downland and the stones themselves, larger and more numerous than we could have imagined. We sat on the top of the bank with a picnic for breakfast, watching as the shadows gradually moved and grew smaller as the sun climbed higher. Then we went exploring – for on this early morning we had the place to ourselves –

Anglo-Saxon dress at Sutton Hoo, Suffolk.

the kids playing hide-and-seek among the stones, which towered impressively over us all.

Part of a rare and extensive Neolithic and Bronze Age landscape, Avebury stone circle is the largest of its kind in the world. The main circle encloses two smaller circles along with most of the village, in which there's a National Trust manor, museum and café. There's so much more to explore nearby too: wander around West Kennet Avenue and Long Barrow; marvel at Silbury Hill, a 30m (98ft) prehistoric mound that was built by hand, or venture a couple of miles down the road to the spectacular downland ridge at Cherhill with its resident white horse, carved into the chalky hillside – one of eight such horses still visible in this part of Wiltshire.

Heading north, to Northumberland, Hadrian's Wall illustrates exceptionally well the vision and work ethic of the Romans. Stretching across the rolling hills in both directions as far as the eye can see, the wall is an extraordinary piece of history that it's impossible to forget. There are many other adventures to be had here too: gaze up at the vast canopy of stars that twinkle across the 572 miles^2 (1,480km^2) of the International Dark Sky Park or try rock climbing at the nearby Crag Lough.

GREAT FOR

HISTORY • YOUNGER KIDS

FASCINATING FACTS

- The Anglo-Saxon burial mounds at Sutton Hoo, Suffolk, concealed more than just the remains of the royalty of the time: two ships and a horse have also been found!
- The stone circle at Avebury, Wiltshire, is the largest of its kind in the world.

TOP TIPS

- If you can, tie in visits with topics children are studying at school. There's nothing like experiencing history in real life to make it exciting and memorable.
- Morning and evening are incredible times to visit ancient sites that are open from dawn till dusk. Take a picnic and warm clothes along and soak up the magical atmosphere.

Where to go

SOUTH WEST

Avebury Stone Circle

near Marlborough, Wiltshire SN8 1RF

Standing not far from its better-known counterpart, Stonehenge, the World Heritage Site at Avebury is the largest prehistoric stone circle in the world. It partially encloses the pretty village of Avebury. There have been some fascinating archaeological discoveries made here, all of which are documented in the Alexander Keiller Museum in the village. The stones are open from dawn until dusk, making this a perfect place to catch sunrise or sunset.

SOUTH EAST

Sutton Hoo

Tranmer House, Sutton Hoo, Woodbridge, Suffolk IP12 3DJ

The discovery, at Sutton Hoo, of an Anglo-Saxon king along with his ship is considered to be one of the greatest archaeological finds of all time. This beautiful 255-acre estate really makes history exciting, with a full-size reconstruction of the burial chamber and some of the original treasures found with the king.

The reconstructed warrior's helmet at Sutton Hoo, Suffolk.

SOUTH WEST

Chedworth Roman Villa

Yanworth, near Cheltenham, Gloucestershire GL54 3LJ

(in certain areas only)

The tranquil, wildlife-filled Cotswold valley at Chedworth houses one of the grandest Roman villas in Britain. Walking around the beautifully preserved site you can really feel what it would have been like in its day, from the stunning in-situ mosaics to the Nymphaeum water shrine, where offerings have been made for well over a thousand years (today it's mainly coins).

NORTH EAST

Hadrian's Wall and Housesteads Fort

Near Bardon Mill, Hexham, Northumberland NE47 6NN

(at visitor centre)

The wild, ancient landscape at Hadrian's Wall makes it a truly memorable place to visit. Perfect if you're learning about the Romans! The sight of the wall marching across the hills into the distance brings the scale and vision of the undertaking to life. Housesteads Fort provides an intriguing insight into the life of Roman soldiers once stationed there.

32 Be a volunteer

Each year, on Dartmoor, groups of volunteers – including lots of families – get together to clear some of the gorse that grows thickly across the moorland. This important work keeps the land clear for people to enjoy and for wildlife to flourish. It's an enjoyable day out and a great way to give something back to the places where we love spending time.

The National Trust runs family volunteering days all over the country, when you can help out with a range of different projects, all of which benefit the special places where they're held. Children can get involved in clearing and planting gardens, chopping down trees, guiding walks and many more activities that make them feel a useful part of the community, as well as having fun and learning new skills. Have a look at nationaltrust.org.uk/volunteer for some great stories from our volunteers.

Joining in with a Big Beach Clean is a fantastic way to turn the growing problem of litter into an opportunity to bring families and communities together, have fun and exercise, help wildlife and feel a great sense of achievement at a worthwhile job well done, all at the same time. And you never know what you might find… Here are some strange things that have been picked up in the past during the National Trust's Beach Cleans:

- bits of a BMW
- parts of an old cooking range, probably from old cottages washed away in the early 1900s
- a scaffold clamp, probably from a Second World War beach defence barrier
- an unbroken light bulb
- a telegraph pole weighing 1 tonne.

You don't have to wait for an organised event, of course, and picking up litter (and remembering not to drop it in the first place) is a great way to teach kids about their responsibility to their surroundings and the direct impact their actions can have on the world around them. Making them aware of the dangers caused by discarded items and the damage it causes to people and wildlife, as well as noticing how unsightly it looks, is an important part of changing behaviours and tackling the problem longer term. And it's incredibly satisfying to make such a positive difference too.

Volunteers collecting rubbish from the beach at Brean Down, North Somerset.

GREAT FOR **GREEN • ACTIVE**

TOP TIPS

- Volunteering is an enjoyable way to make a big difference to a place, learn new skills and meet new people. The National Trust website details all of the opportunities available across the country.

FUN FACT

- The National Trust has over 60,000 volunteers who contribute over 3 million hours of their time each year.

Where to go

SOUTH EAST

White Horse Hill

Dragon Hill Road, Uffington, Oxfordshire SN7 7UK

The Bronze Age horse that can be seen for miles around, leaping across the chalk escarpment of the Ridgeway National Trail, is part of a unique complex of ancient remains to be found in this area. There are Neolithic burial mounds, an Iron Age hill fort and the Giant's Steps: 'ripples' created in the hillside by retreating permafrost during the last Ice Age. Twice a year, on a Sunday, you can go along and help with re-chalking to keep the horse shining bright.

NATIONWIDE

Big Beach Clean

Join in at beaches all over the country to keep them clean and safe for everyone to enjoy. Find full details of your nearest event online at nationaltrust.org.uk.

SOUTH WEST

Arlington Court

Arlington, near Barnstaple, Devon EX31 4LP

Nestled on the edge of Exmoor, Arlington Court is a great place to spot wildlife, with two species of bat, a heronry and a bird hide. During the summer you can join in with a Family Ranger Day: a brilliant opportunity to help the rangers with their work, find out what they do and learn some great skills too. Activities include animal tracking, bug hunting, nature art, pond dipping, pizza making, den building and fire lighting.

Left: Re-chalking the white horse at Uffington.

Above: A Big Beach Clean in Devon.

33 Go on a bat walk

Bats are unlike anything else – literally – being the only mammal that can fly. These curious creatures are fascinating to watch; venturing out just before darkness falls to witness their acrobatic displays as they chase insects for food is always a great adventure. In the past, bats roosted in trees and caves, but increasingly they can be found in the eaves of old buildings, barns, tunnels, churches and bridges. Bats are protected by law, so it's illegal to disturb their roosts in any way. Many National Trust places hold bat walks: group excursions to well-known bat habitats led by local bat experts.

We joined an organised bat walk on a visit to Malham Tarn Estate in the Yorkshire Dales. It was exciting leaving the campsite just as it was getting dark and meeting the throng of waiting families, ready to discover and learn all about the local resident bats. After a general talk on the UK's bat population we walked up a long, rocky track, the kids running around together, enjoying being out in the warm evening air. We arrived at the roost – an old barn high on the estate, not far from Malham Tarn – just before the bats started to fly. Each of us was equipped with a bat detector: a small black box with a dial on it to change the frequency, set to detect the common pipistrelles we would be seeing. For the first ten minutes or so we stood around excitedly, pointing our detectors up at the eaves from which we'd been told the bats would emerge. Eventually, a bat crawled out, still sleepy and slow-moving. After a moment it launched itself into the night sky and flew in fast, high circles above our heads, catching its feast of flying insects. A few emerged more slowly, but, before long, there were hundreds popping in and out from the rafters, fluttering all around us, making the detectors click rapidly, almost wherever we pointed them.

There are organised bat walks at National Trust properties all over the country, throughout the summer months – search online for a comprehensive list or check in your local National Trust newsletter to find one near you. They're great for younger children, who seem to find everything hugely exciting before

FASCINATING FACTS

- Bats are the only mammals that can fly.
- There are 18 different species of bat in the UK.
- The common pipistrelle bat weighs an average of just 5g – that's about the same as a 20p piece!

falling fast asleep! Due to their locations some may not be suitable for buggies (although they're perfect if you have a child-carrier), so check when you book.

A pipistrelle bat. These are the smallest bats found in Europe.

GREAT FOR

WILDLIFE • NATURE • ACTIVE • YOUNGER CHILDREN

TOP TIPS

- Bats are most active at night and don't like cold weather. The best time to spot them is a summer evening, just before it gets dark, near to water or woodland.
- Different bat species communicate using different sounds – or frequencies. Using a bat detector device enables you to tell the difference.
- Many National Trust places hold organised bat walks where you can go to spot bats with a team of experts – an exciting adventure for all age groups.

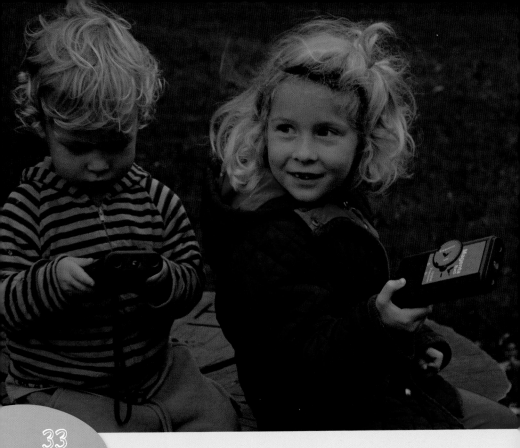

Where to go

YORKSHIRE

Malham Tarn Estate

Waterhouses, Settle, North Yorkshire BD24 9PT

High in the Yorkshire Dales National Park, Malham Estate is a magical place to explore, with limestone pavements, stepped dry valleys and coves created by ancient waterflow and a rich variety of wildlife. There are regular walks from the Malham Tarn Estate Office where, accompanied by a bat detector and resident expert, you can discover the night-time habits of these fascinating creatures. No dogs are allowed on the bat walks.

Using bat detectors on a bat walk at Dyrham Park, Gloucestershire.

SOUTH WEST

Saltram

Plympton, Plymouth, Devon PL7 1UH

Overlooking the River Plym and visible across the water as an enticing green space as you drive into Plymouth, the Saltram Estate is a place of rolling parkland and tranquil woods. It's a great place to spot wildlife, particularly in the evenings, when you'll see bats fluttering through the air and foxes trotting through the grass.

WALES

Stackpole

near Pembroke, Pembrokeshire SA71 5DQ

Stackpole is a hub for outdoor activities, with kayaking, surfing, rock climbing, coasteering and sea swimming nearby. It's also a great place to see all kinds of wildlife, from the otters at Bosherston Lily Ponds to the 12 species of bat that live here, including the largest colony of greater horseshoe bats in Wales. Stay at the campsite (not National Trust) or one of the holiday cottages and you can spend your evenings spotting them as they fly from roosts in eaves and trees across the estate.

34 Go camping

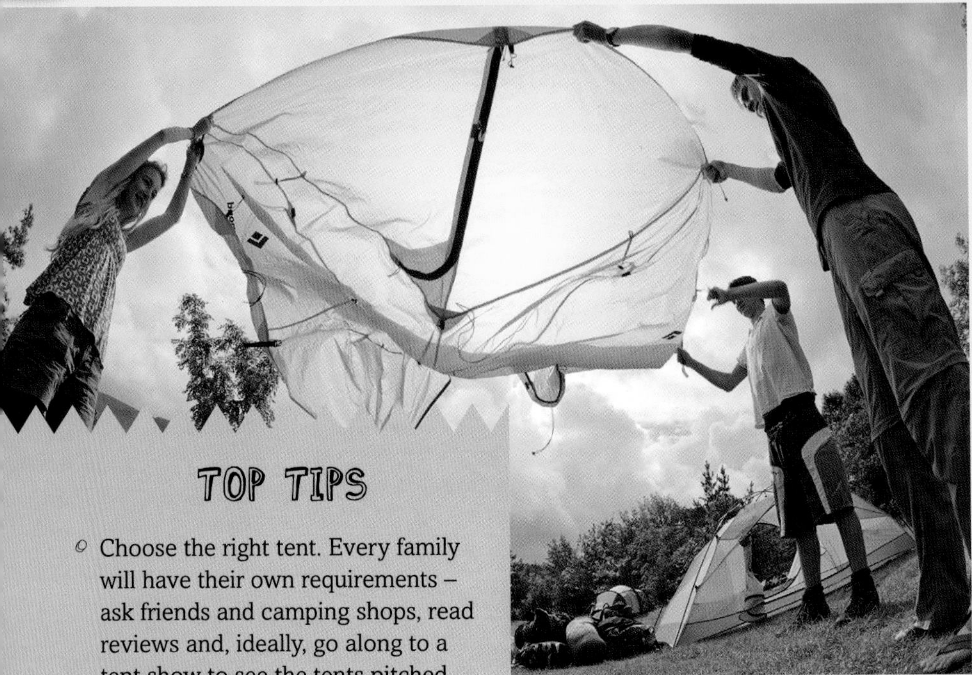

TOP TIPS

- Choose the right tent. Every family will have their own requirements – ask friends and camping shops, read reviews and, ideally, go along to a tent show to see the tents pitched before you decide.
- If it's the first time you've used your tent have a practice run in the garden before you do it for real – it's nice to feel like you know what you're doing once you get to the campsite.
- Take some entertainment along with you – things like Frisbees, footballs, books and games are great for evenings at the campsite or rainy days.
- Get the kids involved with planning your trip – choosing the campsite, deciding on the activities and even meal planning.

A family camping trip can be a perfect way to spend time all together, away from the pressures and distractions of everyday life, in the great outdoors somewhere breathtakingly beautiful. And camping is good for us all: according to a recent study by Plymouth University, children who camp in the great outdoors at least once a year do better at school, and are happier and healthier, and that's definitely a recipe for happy parents too.

Tent pitching in Wasdale campsite, Cumbria.

Family camping's a sociable affair; we rarely saw our eldest when we camped for a fortnight at the National Trust's Great Langdale campsite in the Lake District. The family field is laid out so that the tents form a large circle around a wooded play area in the centre. Kids of all ages seem to get along well here, climbing trees and balancing on obstacles; or they can spend their days playing in the small stream that runs through the site. As with many of the Trust's campsites there's a well-stocked shop for any essentials – or just fresh croissants for breakfast. A beautiful walk down the Great Langdale valley takes you to the Sticklebarn – the only National Trust-run pub and a great place to relax with a cool drink and a pub snack after a long day playing in the hills. There are also lots of organised activities nearby, from ghyll scrambling and rock climbing to bushcraft and foraging.

GREAT FOR

HOLIDAYS • NATURE • ACTIVE

If you're new to camping or fancy something a bit different that's great for the whole family try the National Trust-run annual Big Camp Weekends at various locations nationally. These activity-packed weekends give you the opportunity to experience some of the Trust's incredible places after dark. Pitch your tent, then join in the fun with the other families, playing games or learning how to use a map and compass. After a shared supper there are campfire stories, marshmallow toasting and a spot of star gazing before snuggling down to spend the night under canvas. The following morning join your new friends for breakfast before heading out on a guided walk or taking part in other family-friendly activities.

Watching the sun set over the Peak District.

Where to go

Camping at Great Langdale in the Lake District.

1. Castle Ward, County Down
2. Clumber Park, Nottinghamshire
3. Crom, County Fermanagh
4. Dolaucothi Gold Mine, Carmarthenshire
5. Golden Cap Estate, Dorset
6. Highertown Farm, Cornwall
7. Lake District, Cumbria:
   a. Low Wray, Windermere
   b. Great Langdale
   c. Wasdale
   d. Hoathwaite, Coniston
8. Polesden Lacey, Surrey
9. Saddlescombe Farm, East Sussex
10. Slindon Estate, West Sussex
11. Teneriffe Farm, Cornwall
12. Waterclose Meadows, Cambridgeshire
13. Prattshayes, Exmouth, Devon

England and Wales
Great Langdale
Low Wray
Wasdale
Hoathwaite
Clumber Park
Waterclose
Dolaucothi
Slindon Estate
Polesden Lacey
Saddlescombe Farm
Golden Cap
Prattshayes
Highertown Farm
Teneriffe Farm
Northern Ireland
Crom
Castle Ward

A STEP FURTHER: GREAT ADVENTURES IN WILD PLACES

Aimed at families with older children, or those who love a bigger challenge, this chapter takes you on some really exciting adventures. Swim and sleep in the wild; explore with paddles or pedals; summit a mountain or land on an uninhabited island – and learn the essential survival skills you'll need to help you on your way.

35 An island adventure

Escaping to an island is the stuff of childhood dreams. There's something about a secret place, only accessible on a boat or even a helicopter, which taps deep into our desire for wildness and adventure.

So much about Brownsea Island in Dorset feels wild and adventurous. Whether you're there for a day trip or – as we were – for a longer stay, stepping aboard the boat and heading across the water towards the wooded island that lies nestled in Poole Harbour is an exciting way to begin. Although it's just a short trip from Sandbanks or Poole, it feels like a different world. Island life is incredibly peaceful, with just a few residents who work on Brownsea and two holiday cottages perched right at the water's edge. It has a fascinating history, from factories to recluses to a private holiday destination, and was also the site of Baden-Powell's first scout camp.

Now entirely owned by the National Trust, the island is a nature reserve and SSSI, where no cars or dogs or even bicycles are allowed. Red squirrels scutter up trees or sit on fallen boughs, feasting noisily. You can get quite close, if you're quiet – close enough to see their hairy ears and fluffy tails. There's a fascinating mixture of wildlife here: deer bound across clearings; the strange call of a peacock echoes through the woods; chickens scratch happily in the dust; and wood ants busy themselves about their huge, piled nests. A mixture of beach and sandy cliff edges the island, and here and on the lakes you'll find a vast number of water birds. Oystercatchers, with their matching red beaks and legs, run about on the sand and terns plummet into the sea. There's even a heronry, where you can spot grey herons and little egrets.

Brownsea is only 1½ miles long and a little under a mile wide (2.4 x 1.6km), but it's so varied and there's so much to see and explore that it feels much bigger when you're on it. There's a network of

Walkers by the shore of Derwentwater, Cumbria.

GREAT FOR YOUNGER KIDS • NATURE • ACTIVE

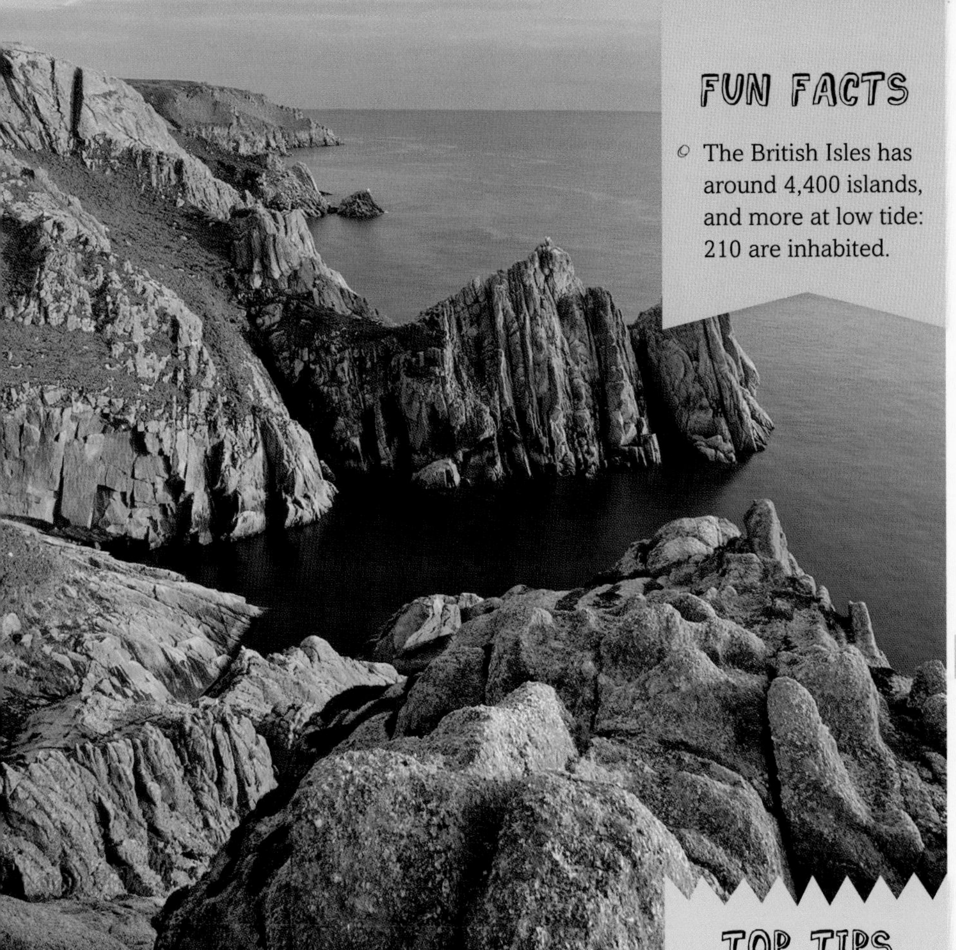

FUN FACTS

- The British Isles has around 4,400 islands, and more at low tide: 210 are inhabited.

TOP TIPS

- Islands are a perfect place for adventures: swimming, kayaking, exploring caves, climbing trees, wild camping… the list is endless. See how many adventures you can fit onto one island!

well-maintained trails so you can visit all the publically accessible parts of the island with ease, even with a buggy. The National Trust has a fleet of excellent all-terrain buggies available to borrow for free. All-in-all it is a perfect place for families – especially those with younger children.

The National Trust owns several islands around the country, many of which make excellent venues for a memorable family adventure. Those you can visit are listed on page 158.

Lundy Island, Devon, which is famous for its puffins.

Where to go

SOUTH WEST

Lundy, Devon

Set in the Bristol Channel, 12 miles (19km) off the coast of North Devon, Lundy is owned by the National Trust but all accommodation on the island is booked through the Landmark Trust. It's a wild place with lots of wildlife to spot and adventures to be discovered. Accessible by boat or helicopter, there's a campsite and pub.

SOUTH EAST

Northey Island, Essex

Walk across the causeway at low tide or otherwise take a boat; this is the closest you'll find to wilderness in Essex. You'll need to ring for a permit and there are no facilities. Once a year you can be a castaway and join other families for a weekend of camping.

SOUTH WEST

Brownsea Island, Dorset

An adventurers' hideaway: a wooded island with much to see and do, from the wild play area to red squirrels scampering up the trees. Jump on a boat from Sandbanks or Poole. Two holiday cottages but no overnight stays otherwise.

NORTH EAST

Lindisfarne, Northumberland

Drive across the tidal causeway – once you're on the island there's a magnificent castle and a wild and windswept landscape to explore. Check the causeway times online before you travel.

NORTHERN IRELAND

Carrick-a-Rede, County Antrim

Cross the rope bridge that's suspended 100ft (30m) above the sea to reach an island of glorious views and fascinating wildlife, including dolphins, porpoises and basking sharks.

NORTH WEST

Derwent Island, Cumbria

Open five days each year, visitors kayak to the island for a tour, time to explore and refreshments. The other three islands on Derwentwater are uninhabited and free for you to land on and explore. NB: no overnight stays or fires.

The rope bridge to Carrick-a-Rede, County Antrim.

36 Track a wild animal

Watching wildlife at St Anthony Head, Cornwall.

The ability to track a wild animal is a little like learning a new language, and once you know how to interpret the signs you come across you can tell a lot about the creature that made them. Tracking wild animals through their natural habitat is a great way to learn many things, from patience and observation to the specific and differing habits of each creature. Here are our top tips for a successful tracking adventure:

Pick your spot

You'll have a much better chance of finding the animal you're looking for if you wait for it in one of its favourite places. Spend some time familiarising yourself with the area, looking for signs of habitation. These could be well-worn paths, visible footprints, new droppings, freshly dug earth or previous sightings. Then focus on these areas when you're tracking the animal.

Take a moment

Find a place to sit where you have a good view of everything going on around you but you're not too obvious. At the bottom of a tree – or even up in its branches – is a good place. Then simply be quiet for a little while, not trying to hear or see anything but allowing your surroundings to forget you're there and return to normal.

Tune in

As you wait, start to take note of the sounds and smells of your surroundings. Birds are good clues to whether there's something about as they'll fly away or make alarm calls. You might be able to hear the crackling of twigs or rustling of leaves as an animal moves around, or even hear it snuffling loudly as we did one evening when we came face-to-face with a big male badger.

Know your target

To be in with the best chance of actually seeing a wild animal, get familiar with its habits. Foxes will leave droppings in prominent places; badgers will use the same paths every night; otters leave fish bones and claw marks in the muddy riverbank; deer make 'couches' – flattened areas where they lie down.

Be observant

Knowing what to look for and spotting the tiniest clues are the keys to success when you're tracking: look for hairs left on fences and plants; footprints in mud or snow; snapped, chewed or trampled vegetation and droppings. Fresh earth around holes means they're likely still to be in use.

It's not always easy to see wild animals, but it's exciting tracking them down and working out their clues. If you don't find one on the first attempt, try again. And above all, explore and have fun!

Wild grasses and empty beaches at Murlough National Nature Reserve, County Down.

TOP TIPS

- Many of Britain's wild animals are nocturnal (active at night) or crepuscular (active at twilight), so these are good times to go tracking.

Where to go

WALES

Penrhyn Castle

Bangor, Gwynedd LL57 4HT

Penrhyn is a nineteenth-century neo-Norman castle that's fun to explore along with its garden and parkland. There's a railway museum here where you can learn about locomotives and the local quarry. Lying on the wild northern edge of Snowdonia, it's a great place to track the many creatures that live around here. There are organised Wild Nature Days when you can join an expert to spot, identify and follow animal tracks and learn how to attract wild creatures to your own garden.

EAST OF ENGLAND

Wicken Fen National Nature Reserve

Lode Lane, Wicken, Ely, Cambridgeshire CB7 5XP

Wicken Fen is one of Europe's most important wetlands with more than 8,500 species, including an amazing variety of plants, birds and insects. Follow the raised boardwalks to discover the secret world of the wild creatures that live here. There are lots of organised activities here, including bat walks, pond dipping and minibeast hunts. You can cycle, walk or take a boat ride – and even sleep under the stars at the special 'wild' campsite in open-fronted log shelters – no tent required!

NORTHERN IRELAND

Murlough National Nature Reserve

Keel Point, Dundrum, County Down BT33 0NQ

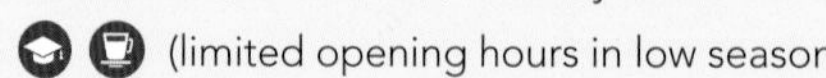

(limited opening hours in low season)

An internationally important nature reserve created on 6,000-year-old sand dunes, Murlough has an abundance of wildlife from waterfowl to wildflower meadows. Bordered by the sea and the rugged Mourne Mountains it's a breathtakingly beautiful place to be. There are self-guided nature trails.

Family of Canada Geese at Calke's National Nature Reserve, Derbyshire.

37 Climb a mountain

Mountains are places of myth and legend; the dwelling-places of giants and dragons, high up above the clouds. The mountainous areas of Britain are a whole new world to be explored, and the weather, terrain and challenges are on a different scale to those at sea-level. A great family adventure can be found by picking a mountain – or an interesting-looking hill – and attempting to reach the summit. It's fun to explore the map together, finding heights and footpaths, sifting out those that have potential and finally deciding on the right one. Setting out, fully equipped for the day, the route planned but the whole experience still to come, is incredibly exciting. The climb is often hard work, but always rewarding, and it's important to stop and regather from time to time on your way up – to refuel and look back along the way you've come and see the height you've gained. There's the brilliant moment when the summit finally appears and you can stop and take in the views. Summits are special places; we've had many interesting conversations on the tops of mountains with others who have made the same ascent and shared similar experiences. There are not so many things so straightforward in concept yet utterly rewarding as climbing a mountain – and getting back down again of course because, as all aspiring mountaineers know, the top is only half way.

Weather and geography play a big part in mountain environments, so factor these in when planning your adventure. Winter and poor weather raises the level of challenge considerably, with excellent navigational and survival skills and specialist equipment necessary for many upland areas.

FUN FACTS

- In Britain, a mountain is any high point over 610m (2,000ft) above sea-level with at least 30m (100ft) of ascent on all sides.
- There are 179 mountains in England, 138 in Wales and 19 in Northern Ireland.
- These mountains are sometimes known as HEWITTs, which stands for Hill in England, Wales or Ireland over Two Thousand feet.

GREAT FOR

BIG ADVENTURES • NATURE • ACTIVE

Your 'mountain' doesn't have to be an official one, of course. Any interesting-looking hill can be an adventure, and younger children often like to be able to see the summit from the start so that they know how far they've gone and how far there is to go. Start small and, as they grow, so will the mountains they can climb.

TOP TIPS

- Plan your route carefully, including options for retreat.
- Pack plenty of food, water and spare clothing – take a look at the advice on pages 7–13.
- Don't forget to take a summit photo!

Family mountain adventures and the all-essential summit picture!

37
Climb a mountain

Where to go

WALES

Sugar Loaf and Skirrid Fawr

Sugar Loaf: Brecon Beacons, Abergavenny, Monmouthshire NP7 7LA
Skirrid Fawr: Llanwerth car park, Abergavenny, Monmouthshire NP7 8AP

A picture-perfect mountain (although at 486m/1,600ft not quite tall enough to be an official HEWITT) that rises out of the beautiful Usk Valley in the Black Mountains range. Skirrid is a great starter summit for first-time mountaineers or younger children, but it's still a great day out with some more challenging options to suit all ages and abilities. Neighbouring Sugar Loaf stands 596m (1,955ft) high, with a very achievable walk to the summit for spectacular views out across the Brecon Beacons.

NORTH WEST

Stickle Ghyll

Great Langdale, near Ambleside, Cumbria LA22 9JU

Starting next to the Sticklebarn, the only National Trust-run pub, the adventurous trail that follows Stickle Ghyll up the mountainside to the gleaming shores of Stickle Tarn is a brilliant adventure. It's generally straightforward walking, but there are a few fairly large step-ups that small children may require help with. When you reach the top, jump in the tarn for a refreshing paddle before heading back down or carry on past the face of Pavey Ark to reach High Raise at 762m (2,500ft).

Top right: Starting the climb up Mam Tor in the Peak District, Derbyshire.
Right: At the summit of Sugar Loaf in the Brecon Beacons, Monmouthshire.

EAST MIDLANDS

Mam Tor

near Castleton, Derbyshire S33 8WA

Standing at 517m (1,695ft) high, the summit of Mam Tor is one of the most dramatic viewpoints in the Peak District. From the summit you can see out over the Edale Valley to Kinder Scout and the Derwent Moors, or on a clear night it's a wonderful spot for stargazing. The walk is about half a mile (0.8km) from the car park, along clear, well-trodden paths and steps to the summit, where an ancient hill fort awaits exploration.

38 Wilderness survival and bushcraft

Learning bushcraft and wilderness survival skills is the ultimate way to feel more connected with nature. The confidence that comes with having the knowledge to create shelter, fire and food with nothing but the natural materials around you makes wild places friendlier, less intimidating and even more exciting. One of the best ways to learn these skills is to go on a family bushcraft weekend: an amazing adventure that gets families working and playing together, doing something different and learning all about their beautiful surroundings, guided by passionate and knowledgeable experts.

Bushcraft activities can be tailored to suit any age – even babies enjoy watching the flames flicker in a campfire. Pre-schoolers love building dens and playing with the naturally available art materials in the woods: sticks, mud and leaves. Kids really start getting excited about the idea of surviving in the wilderness around the age of seven, when they have enough manual dexterity to wield a knife safely, are happy to sleep alone in a hammock or shelter, and have the patience for things

Making a den at Sheringham Park, Norfolk.

requiring a bit more tenacity like lighting fires without matches.

National Trust Lake District partners Woodmatters (www.woodmatters.org.uk) work in Cumbria alongside communities to recognise and celebrate the emotional, physical and environmental benefits from healthy, sustainable woodlands. Their woodland immersion camps 'aim to inspire a deepening of people's connection with Nature, enabling a gentle introduction to woodland life whilst learning core bushcraft, natural arts, Nature ID and survival skills'.

A typical weekend itinerary might include the following:

Tuning in – find a quiet space nestled against a tree and allow your senses to explore and slow down to the pace of woodland life.
Firelighting – learning safe and effective methods using basic fire steels and natural tinders.
Knife skills – how to use sharp tools safely and whittle interesting things such as spoons, whistles, bows and arrows, and candlesticks. You'll also learn how to make useful cord from natural materials – essential for building in the woods.
Create your woodland bed – either by building a shelter to sleep under or pitching your hammock and tarp, ready for a night under the stars.
Nature identification – tracking and naming woodland animals and identifying useful and edible plants.
Campfire dinner – cooking over flames in the woods, with stories and treats.
Sleeping in the woodland – and waking up to birds singing, a campfire breakfast and another day of adventures…

TOP TIPS

- Great bushcraft adventures start at home! Try throwing a tarp over the washing line in your garden as a shelter, or light a campfire in a firebowl or barbecue base and spend an evening around it, toasting marshmallows and telling stories.

Bushcraft activities at Footprint, Cumbria.

GREAT FOR

LEARNING • NATURE • ACTIVE

Where to go

NORTH WEST

Footprint

St Catherine's, Patterdale Road, Windermere, Cumbria LA23 1NH
(Facilities and parking for those booked in)

A 20-minute walk from Windermere station, Footprint is a straw-bale building made to provide a space for learning. All sorts of nature-based classes are run here, including Woodmatters' bushcraft weekends.

EAST MIDLANDS

Kedleston Hall

near Quarndon, Derby, Derbyshire DE22 5JH

Kedleston Hall is a grand, eighteenth-century mansion that starred in Hollywood blockbuster *The Duchess*. There's always lots going on for families, from bushcraft and family volunteering days to pre-school and home-educators' groups.

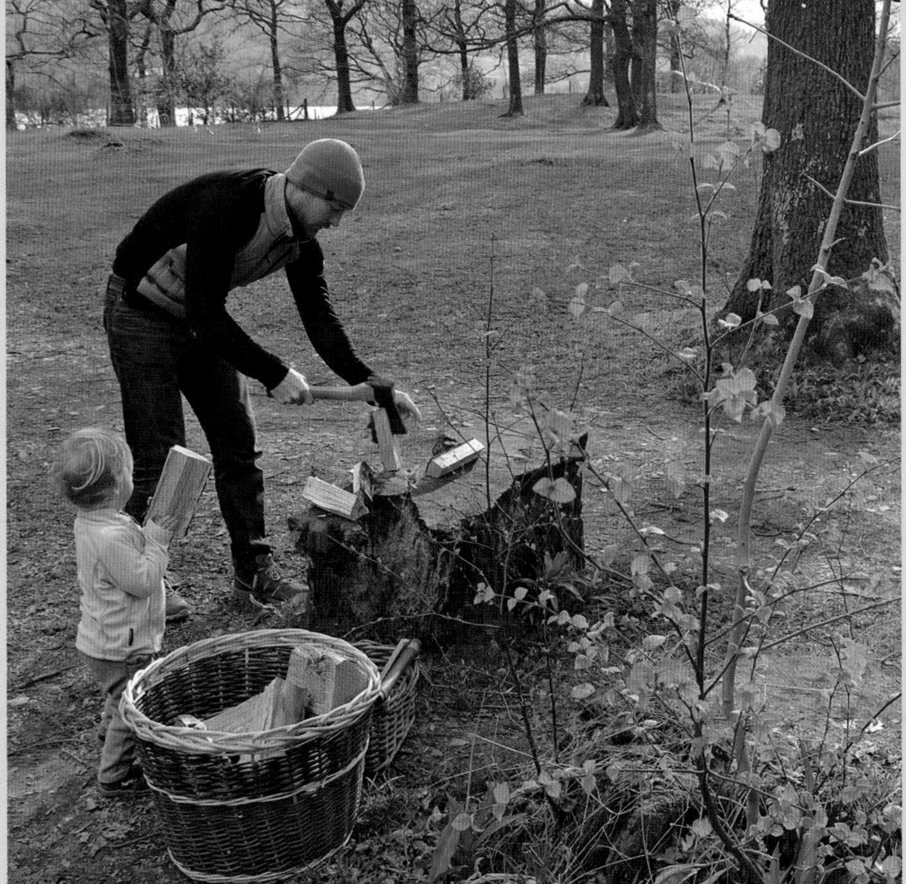

NORTH EAST

Gibside

near Rowlands Gill, Gateshead, Tyne & Wear NE16 6BG

A crumbling Georgian masterpiece, Gibside is being gently restored with families and children firmly in mind. There are three adventure play areas, kid-friendly options in the café and shop, and you can borrow a top-of-the-range off-road buggy if you fancy a walk (or run) around the beautiful estate. There's plenty of opportunity for learning too, with bushcraft, orienteering, archery and more to join in with.

Above: Chopping firewood at Low Wray, Cumbria.

Left: Getting cosy in a hammock at Footprint, Cumbria.

39 Go bouldering

TOP TIPS

- A bouldering mat is effectively a crash pad, and a great investment for keen boulderers. They are usually made of several layers of lightweight foam and fold in half, with a strap for carrying. They make falling off boulders much more enjoyable.
- Always inspect the landing when bouldering – sand and grass are great, but use a mat to cover any rocks.
- Wear a good pair of grippy shoes, ideally specialised rock shoes, to help you stand on the smallest holds.

Bouldering in the Peak District.

Bouldering – climbing lower routes without ropes – is a perfect introduction to rock climbing. It's simple and relatively low-cost to start, requiring only a pair of rock shoes, a chalk bag and a bouldering mat, whether you're a beginner or experienced. There are many classic places to go bouldering, usually popular due to ease of access, an abundance of interesting rock formations and the type of rock, ideally being solid – i.e. not prone to breaking off – and with a good level of friction. Rock types vary between locations and lend an area its characteristics: Dartmoor's granite is rough and crystalline; the Peak District's gritstone is rounded and high-friction; the Lakes' rhyolite and the many limestone regions offer well-featured climbing with plenty of edges for hand- and foot-holds.

Bouldering is a great family activity as it caters for all levels of age and ability. It's a sociable sport that lends itself well to group days out, and usually takes you to beautiful places; so when you've had enough of clambering around on the rocks you can always sit in the sunshine and admire the scenery.

Boulder problems are graded according to their level of challenge, but you can start out by simply having a go

GREAT FOR CHALLENGES • NATURE • ACTIVE

at scrambling up any interesting-looking rocks. Grading scales vary across the country, but in general the higher the number the more difficult the problem. 'V' grades are common and fairly straightforward, starting at V0 and going all the way up to V13. Although most good bouldering venues have a range of problems at different levels of difficulty, some are more beginner-friendly than others.

FUN FACTS

- Bouldering is a fun, low-cost way of learning the skills needed for rock climbing. It does not require ropes and usually takes place on smaller rocks with shorter, lower climbs.
- You don't have to go outside – if it's a rainy day you could always head to one of the UK's many indoor climbing or bouldering venues to hone your skills and techniques ready for the real thing.

Where to go

EAST MIDLANDS

Burbage South, Derbyshire

www.peakbouldering.info

Just outside Sheffield in the Peak District, the gritstone boulders at Burbage have plenty of easier-grade problems with good, grassy landings.

NORTH WEST

St Bees, Cumbria

(not National Trust)

www.lakesbloc.com

A wonderful day out at the seaside with dozens of sculpted sandstone boulders to play on.

Great Langdale, Cumbria

Head for the Langdale Boulders or, at the National Trust campsite, there's a purpose-built traversing wall.

WALES

RAC boulders, Snowdonia, Gwynedd

(not National Trust)

www.northwalesbouldering.com

Lots of easier-grade bouldering with magnificent views, all within a short walk of the car park.

SOUTH WEST

Hound Tor, Dartmoor, Devon

(not National Trust)

www.javu.co.uk

Scramble right to the top of the tower of granite blocks or play on one of many lower down, high on the open moor.

Spotting a boulderer in the Peak District.

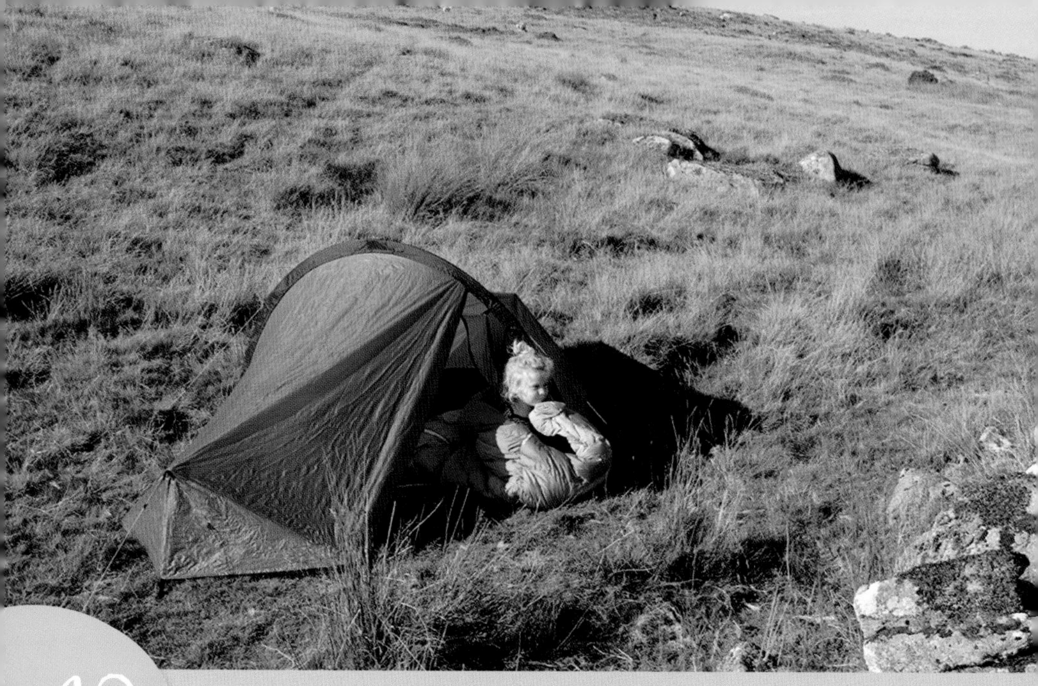

40 Camp in the wild

There really is nothing quite like going wild camping. It's a complete escape in so many ways, from having the freedom to choose where you sleep to being completely self-sufficient – if only for a night. Even if you don't walk far before you set up camp, a night camping wild always feels like a proper adventure.

With a little planning the first time, regular wild camping expeditions are a brilliant way to get some 'wild time', sleeping outside with nature all around. Start with some careful packing, deciding what you really need and what you can probably do without, and then attempting to fit it all into one rucksack. Then there's the really exciting part of finding a pitch, walking across a wild moorland landscape, searching for the perfect spot. Look for soft, springy grass to lie on; shelter from the wind; a place hidden from view; a nearby stream... And, of course, the view you want to wake up to in the morning. As evening falls, pitch the tent – the kids love to get involved, handing out pegs and making beds. Make sure you're well away from roads and houses, and clear any twigs or rocks away so you don't damage your groundsheet (or your knees). Then snuggle into your sleeping bag with the soft darkness of night-time on the hills and the hooting of owls to lull you to sleep. It's a delicious thing to wake up to dawn birdsong, breakfast with a view and – if you're lucky – a spectacular sunrise.

We're lucky enough to have friends who live within Dartmoor National Park, so for our wild camping adventure we stopped in with them for supper and some good advice on the best places to camp first. Poring over the map we spotted a few likely-looking places to spend the night, and mapped out a basic route to get there. With the two of us and the two kids we had two big rucksacks packed to the brim with kit: a lightweight backpacking tent, sleeping bags, roll mats, food, water and a torch as well as plenty of warm clothing. It was the summer solstice so it was still light when we left the house and walked up onto the open moor later in the evening. We found a perfect spot, just below some large rocks with a glorious view out across the valley. It was drizzling as we set up camp, and we went to sleep to the gentle pitter-patter of rain on the tent canvas. The most magical part of the adventure was waking up to a bright, sunny morning and sharing home-made flapjacks in the awning of the tent, gazing out at our view.

FASCINATING FACTS

- True wild camping involves simply finding a spot to camp for the night – and camping!
- Wild camping is allowed in some areas of some National Parks. Dartmoor has a map of areas where you are allowed to wild camp, while the Brecon Beacons have a list of farms that are happy to have wild campers on their land.

Waking up after a night of wild camping.

TOP TIPS

- Pitch your tent at dusk and leave early.
- Leave no trace – take all rubbish with you and don't light fires.
- Pack light – you may need to carry all of your equipment some distance before you find the perfect spot, so don't pack anything you don't need.
- Always follow local guidelines when wild camping.

GREAT FOR WEEKENDER • NATURE • ACTIVE

Where to go

SOUTH WEST

Dartmoor, Devon

(Selected areas only)

Dartmoor is the only national park that explicitly allows wild camping, and this is in specific areas and following clear criteria. Visit the Dartmoor National Park Authority website dartmoor.gov.uk for details.

Pitching the tent in a sheltered spot ready for a night's wild camping.

EAST OF ENGLAND

Wicken Fen wild campsite

Lode Lane, Wicken, Ely, Cambridgeshire CB7 5XP

With an open-fronted log shelter to sleep in, plus a fire pit and a composting loo, you have everything you need for a weekend of wild adventures.

NATIONWIDE

Wild Camp and Big Camp events

National Trust properties across the country hold organised events where you can sleep under the stars and experience special places at night.

41 Paddle your own canoe

Open, Canadian-style canoes are a great place to start when it comes to self-powered explorations on the water. They're stable, easy to control and can fit a whole family. There's little more wonderful than paddling gently down a calm river in the sun, or crossing a lake to have a picnic on a remote and inaccessible shore, then paddling your own canoe back to civilisation. A perfect family adventure!

Low Wray campsite in the Lake District is one of our favourite places for an adventurous family holiday: waking

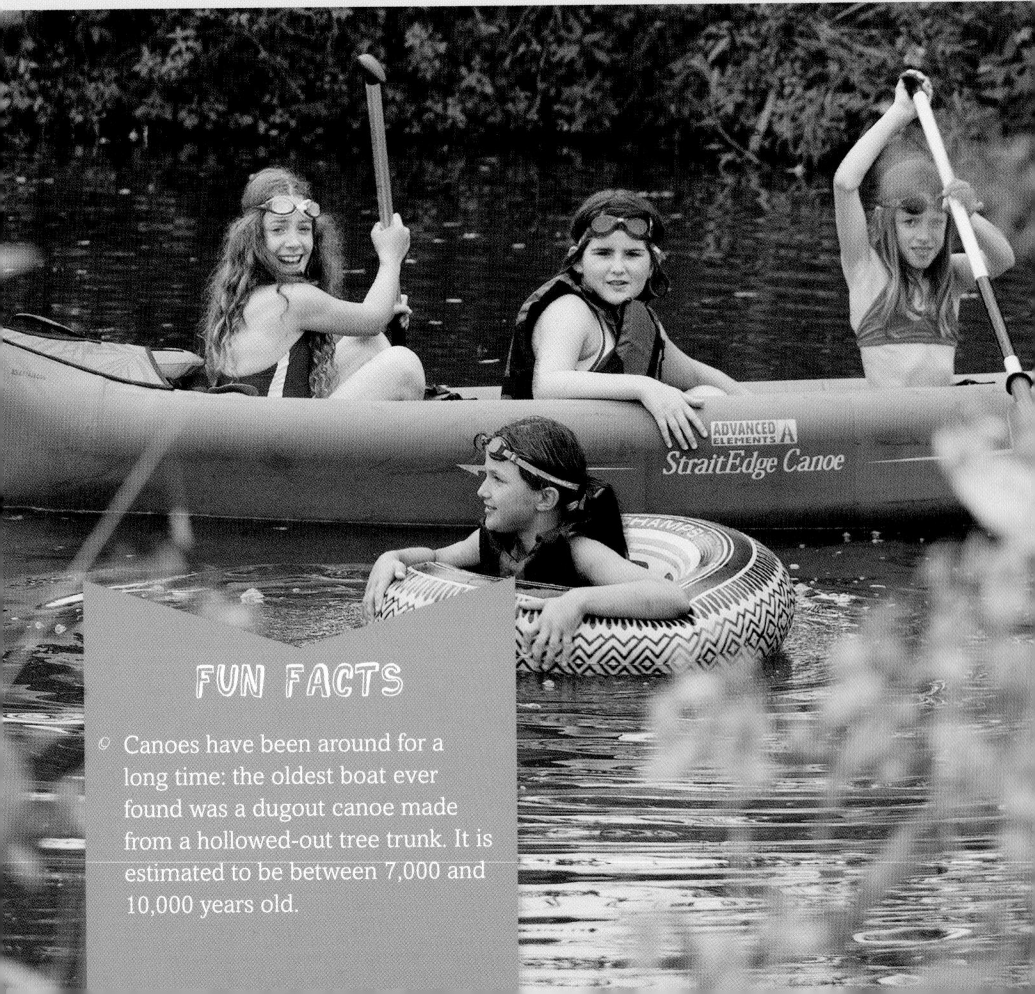

Inflatable canoe fun on the river.

FUN FACTS

- Canoes have been around for a long time: the oldest boat ever found was a dugout canoe made from a hollowed-out tree trunk. It is estimated to be between 7,000 and 10,000 years old.

up on the shores of Windermere to the sounds of water birds and a peaceful view out across the water to the mountains beyond. Wray Castle is just a lakeside stroll away and there's a network of well-marked walking/cycling trails to explore, including one that takes you into nearby Ambleside. You can jump into one of the canoes available to hire at the campsite and paddle off across the serene lake in search of secret islands and hidden coves. Being on the quieter side of Windermere there's little other traffic here other than grebes and mallards and the occasional heron, so it's a perfect introduction to paddling for kids.

Further afield you'll find the National Trust's canoe trails, specifically designed to give you the best kayaking or canoeing tour of an area. These can be found in places such as the picturesque estuary at Salcombe in South Devon, where you can download a map or buy a waterproof version, and magical Strangford Lough, near Belfast, County Down. Strangford Lough is the largest inlet in the UK and Ireland. It's a haven for wildlife and a delight to explore by boat. The seaward side of the lough – 'The Routen Wheel' – is a series of whirlpools, boils and swirling waters, caused by pinnacles of rock on the seabed, and should be treated with extreme caution. Further north, however, are the calm waters of Lough Cuan, a sheltered basin with many routes to explore, surrounded by spectacular scenery and varied wildlife.

TOP TIPS

- It's a good idea to wear a buoyancy aid when you're canoeing, even if you're a strong swimmer. Young children and non-swimmers must wear a life jacket: this will keep them afloat and their airways open even if they're unable to swim.

GREAT FOR

WATER • NATURE • ACTIVE

A canoe safari.

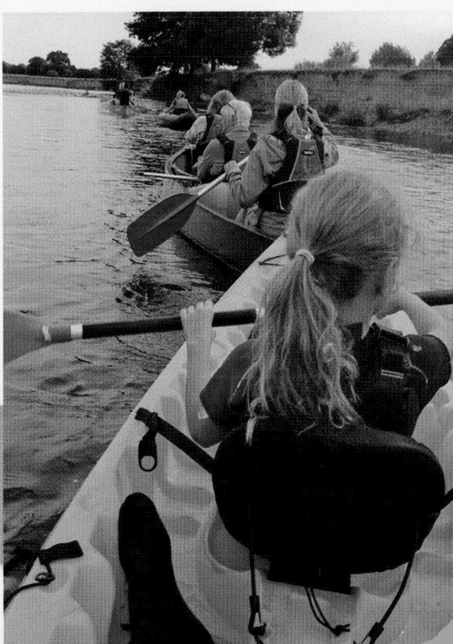

Where to go

NORTH WEST

Derwent Water

Cumbria

Hire a boat or take your own and set off to explore the gleaming lake, wooded banks and secret islands of Derwent Water. There are four islands here: St Herbert's, Derwent, Lord's and Rampsholme. Derwent is the only one that's inhabited, but you can land on and explore any of the others. Don't stay overnight, leave anything on the islands or light fires. Fell Foot, at Windermere, is another great Lake District kayaking location, with lots to do on the water, perfect for families.

NORTHERN IRELAND

Crom

Upper Lough Erne, Newtownbutler, County Fermanagh BT92 8AJ

A hauntingly beautiful ruin and estate on the edge of Upper Lough Erne. There's so much to do here: take a kayak or open canoe out to explore the lough, perhaps paddling over to Belturbet for lunch; hire a rowing or outboard engine boat; camp or glamp at the nearby campsite; see if you can spot a rare pine marten.

SOUTH WEST

Watersmeet, Exmoor

Watersmeet Road, Lynmouth, Devon EX35 6NT

Watersmeet on Exmoor is the meeting place of the East Lyn River and Hoar Oak Water. With its dramatic river gorge and 2,000 acres of countryside and woodland to explore it's a great place to spend the day, wildlife watching and taking in the glorious views. The stretch of river provides enjoyable kayaking for proficient paddlers – but it's not suitable for beginners. You can kayak here between 1 October and 31 March, provided there is enough water. NB: there are set access points to the water – please check website or ask at the visitor centre.

Left: Watersmeet House on the river Lyn.

Below: A family canoe adventure in Devon.

42 Ride a mountain-bike trail

Going on family bike rides is a brilliant way to all get outside together, being active, learning great new skills and exploring new places. From the moment our children could sit up on their own we'd pop them in a bike seat and enjoy the freedom it gave us to have proper adventures again. As they grew bigger they rode four-wheelers, three-wheelers and then balance bikes, and we can't wait until they're big enough to pedal along next to us for long days out on the trails. For the time being a double bike trailer works well – as long as it's not too bumpy!

A group cycle ride on a waymarked cycle trail in Cheshire.

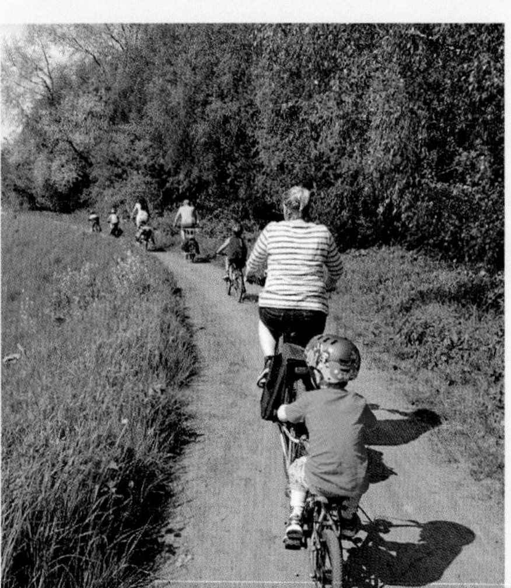

There's nothing quite like riding fast along winding single-track through dense woodland, skipping past trees, taking jumps, corners and descents as they appear. There are many great trails that run through National Trust places, with some being well suited to gentler family bike rides and others offering more of a challenge for the experienced rider.

Leigh Woods, a lush area of deciduous woodland on the plateau above the Avon Gorge near Bristol, is a great place to head if you're after an exciting, challenging ride. There are some excellent purpose-built mountain bike tracks here: the Yer Tiz Trail is an engaging, moderate, 'blue' grade trail that weaves its way through the woodland for just over 2 miles (3.2km). The trail features berms (banked corners), rollers (bumps), drops and climbs, perfect for honing your skills. If you're after something a bit trickier, split off onto the red-graded Gert Lush Trail, a short stretch of narrow, technical trail that's only suitable for experienced riders.

The 20-mile (32km) Win Hill circuit mountain bike trail passes the tranquil Ladybower Reservoir and climbs steeply up from Hope in the Edale Valley in Derbyshire, to where glorious views

GREAT FOR • NATURE • ACTIVE

across the Dark Peak and gentler riding await. There's also a fast, fun, rough descent into the Derwent Valley. A proper adventure that's easily accessible by train from Manchester and Sheffield, this trail would suit families with older children.

For families with younger children or those looking for a gentler day's cycling, many of the Trust's estates have surfaced, well-waymarked trails of varying distances so you can pick the one that suits you. Some of our favourite family cycle trails are: Ashridge Estate in Hertfordshire (5 to 17 miles/8 to 27km); Lanhydrock, Cornwall; Giant's Causeway, Antrim (12 miles/19km) and the Manifold Way in Derbyshire (8 miles/13km). For a longer day out with gentler cycling, there's a stunning 22½-mile (36-km) cycle trail at Coniston in the Lake District or the 20-mile (32km) South Somerset Cycle Trail.

TOP TIPS

- Cycling is a great way to explore for families with children of any age. If your kids aren't yet able to cycle longer distances, many National Trust places have trailers, bike seats or tag-along bikes to hire: perfect for younger explorers.

The Chiltern Hills at Ashridge Estate, Hertfordshire.

Where to go

SOUTH WEST

Leigh Woods, near Bristol

Bristol BS8 3QB

(not National Trust)

Just a short trip from the bustling city of Bristol, Leigh Woods is a haven of leafy tranquillity. The Yer Tiz Trail requires a mountain bike but is suitable for anyone who can ride confidently. There are lots of other family-friendly activities on, such as wilderness survival days and organised tree climbs.

A short break to plan the next section.

EAST OF ENGLAND

Ashridge Estate

Moneybury Hill, Ringshall,
Near Berkhamsted,
Hertfordshire HP4 1LT

Ashridge Estate covers 2,000 acres of the Chiltern Hills. It's criss-crossed by a vast network of trails, perfect for exploring on a mountain bike. Keep your eyes peeled for wildlife, including deer, rare butterflies and wildflowers.

Cycling through the Bramshaw Commons, Hampshire.

SOUTH WEST

Lanhydrock

Bodmin, Cornwall PL30 5AD

By far the best way to explore the delights of the Lanhydrock estate is on a bike. There are six graded trails, from the easy Lodge Trail to the technical and tricky red route, the Saw Pit. There's even a skills area to practise in. Bike hire is available, including trailers – perfect for adventures with younger children.

43 Explore a waterfall

Water is a central theme at the National Trust's dramatic Lydford Gorge, the deepest gorge in the south-west of England. A rocky path edges a river, which in places is a calm and sparkling stream that looks perfect for paddling, yet in others becomes a raging, swirling, gurgling torrent, awe-inspiring and exciting to watch. It's an adventurous walk, not suitable for buggies or those who aren't confident walkers and it's slippery in the wet, but an enjoyable and rewarding challenge for budding explorers. The gorge is packed with wildlife too, with dippers flying low along the water and springtime bringing the woodland alive with fragrant, green wild garlic. We visited after heavy rain, when the swollen river rushed past and the waterfall was at its fullest. We carried our two children on our backs in their carriers, carefully making our way down into the gorge itself, cut deep into the rocky ground by millennia of flowing water. Ducking through caves and inching around boulders we arrived at the White Lady: a delicate white fall that tumbles some 100ft (30m) through the leafy undergrowth into a deep pool below. Finally, traversing a walk suspended high above the chasm, we entered a dark, moss-lined ravine and discovered the Devil's Cauldron: a booming cavern where the water swirls and boils below your feet. Lydford, right on the edge of Dartmoor, is a beautiful place to visit whether or not

White Lady waterfall at Lydford Gorge, Devon.

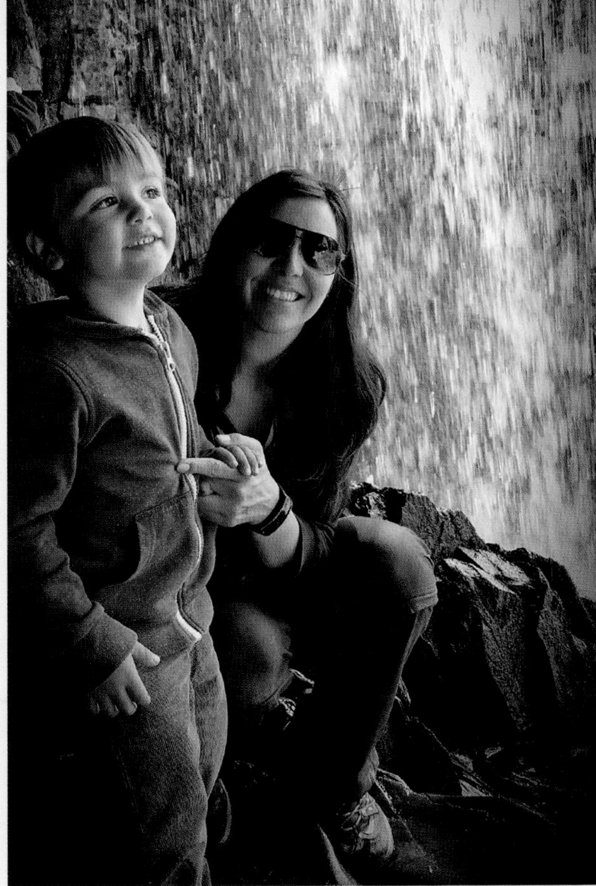

Behind the waterfall.

you're up for the full 3-mile (5km) walk. There's a fantastic adventure playground too!

Aira Force on the edge of Ullswater in the Lake District is another great day out, with kayaking, swimming, paddling and exciting wild walks around an impressive waterfall. You can even arrive by boat in the summer months, with a ride on the Ullswater Steamer. Or, for a really exciting experience, walk through the waterfall at Henrhyd in Powys, the highest waterfall in South Wales. There's a dark cave to explore on the other side (allegedly once visited by Batman), and the air is filled with the sounds and spray from the falls. This is a place that feels truly wild, and the surrounding dense foliage of Graigllech Woods is a haven for wildlife.

FUN FACTS

- The UK's highest waterfall is Eas a' Chual Aluinn in Scotland, which plunges 200m (658ft) in a single drop.
- Angel Falls, in Venezuela, is the highest waterfall in the world, falling an incredible 979m (3,212ft)!

GREAT FOR

CHALLENGING ADVENTURES • NATURE • ACTIVE

TOP TIPS

- Waterfalls vary according to rainfall and tend to be at their most dramatic after heavy rain.
- Visiting a waterfall is a great addition to many other adventures, such as wild swimming, kayaking or caving.

43

Explore a waterfall

Where to go

NORTH WEST

Aira Force

near Watermillock, Penrith, Cumbria CA11 0JS

Peaceful Ullswater, nestled in a valley surrounded by fells, is home to Aira Force: a dramatic waterfall that drops 20m (66ft) through a rocky, wooded gorge. This is wonderful family walking country, with trails winding through ancient woodland and pretty glades. For bigger adventures, take to the lake where you can explore by kayak and go for a wild swim, or simply jump aboard a steamer and take in the spectacular views.

SOUTH WEST

Lydford Gorge

Lydford, near Tavistock, Devon EX20 4BH

The walk around Lydford Gorge is exciting, intriguing and often dramatic, as you make your way along narrow footways, through rocky arches, across bridges and alongside the River Lyd. Particular highlights are the majestic White Lady waterfall, which cascades 100ft (30m) into a deep plunge pool and the roaring Devil's Cauldron. Not suitable for unsteady walkers in places.

WALES

Henrhyd

near Coelbren, Brecon Beacons, Powys
SA10 9PG

At 27m (90ft), Henrhyd Falls is the highest waterfall in South Wales; set deep in a wooded valley in the Brecon Beacons it's an adventure to find. Once you're there it's a delightful, watery glen, with a stream to paddle in, or follow the trail around and stand behind the fall. It can be a little tricky to get behind the falls but the cave behind the water was featured in the film *Batman*: *The Dark Knight Rises* and you can see where the batmobile was hidden away!

Far left: Janet's Foss in Yorkshire Dales National Park. This small waterfall is easy to reach, making it ideal for young families.
Left: Admiring the falls at Lydford Gorge, Devon.

44 Go wild swimming

There's nothing quite like sliding into the cool water of a gently flowing river and letting the current carry you slowly down stream. The unique view afforded by swimming puts you at a level with the creatures that share the water;

TOP TIPS

- Don't swim anywhere with poor or unknown water quality.
- Be aware of sudden deep places and strong currents, and keep a careful eye on smaller children and those who aren't strong swimmers.
- Check for depth and hidden hazards before jumping in.
- Don't get too cold – children especially cool very quickly, so keep a careful eye on them, encourage plenty of running about and have plenty of warm clothing and energy-packed snacks at the ready.
- Be aware of other people using the water, especially anglers and boats.
- Never swim alone or allow children to do so; keep a careful watch and – if possible – go with someone who knows the area well.
- If you're looking for recommendations for the best places to go, try the Wild Swimming books, many of which are available from National Trust shops.

wildlife nearby watch with interest rather than disappearing in fright; a watery world from a 'frog's eye view' as Roger Deakin put it in his book *Waterlog*.

With the right choice of location, wild swimming is an exciting and memorable adventure for children of any age. Paddling barefoot is a great way to introduce them to the water, keeping them safe while allowing them to explore the new sensations that natural water brings. Older children may be happy swimming in deeper sections of river, jumping into plunge pools or riding the waves in the sea.

Woodland streams and rivers provide wonderfully sheltered places to paddle and swim when the sun is hot. One glorious summer day we followed paths that wound through ancient Dartmoor woodland, leaving the busy, easily accessible part of the river behind and venturing into the cool, dappled shade of the trees. A little further on we found an island in the river, where wild whortleberry bushes thickly carpet the ground. Here we spent the day paddling in the shallows, swimming in deep pools, warmed by the recent sun, and feasting on sweet berries.

Left: Jumping the waves.

Above: Fun with an underwater camera.

GREAT FOR

EXTREME • NATURE • ACTIVE

Where to go

NORTHERN IRELAND

Pig Island, Strangford Lough, County Antrim
A sheltered sea swim with parking nearby and glorious views of the Mourne Mountians. At low tide you can wade much of the way to the island, but it gets much deeper when the tide is in. Keep an eye out for windsurfers.

WEST MIDLANDS

Carding Mill Valley, Shropshire
Deep in the Shropshire Hills, this diverse and wildlife-rich area offers lots to see and explore. Paddle in the stream that runs through the valley or swim in the reservoir – but make sure you read the information board first.

NORTH WEST

Wasdale Head, Cumbria
Take the plunge on your own or join a guided swim in the remote and beautiful Wastwater, surrounded by Lake District fells. The best spot for swimming is known locally as the Blue Lagoon – it's a 1.3-mile (2.1km) walk from the parking at Wasdale Head.

SOUTH WEST

Studland Bay, Dorset
Gently shelving and sheltered, Studland is a great place for a first go at sea swimming. There's lots of sand for playing in and the Knoll Beach Café for post-swim refreshments too.

SOUTH EAST

Compton Bay, Isle of Wight
The tide doesn't go too far out here, leaving a good area of shallow water, perfect for sea swimming in relative safety. The beach is great for families too.

A simple rope swing can create hours of fun.

45 Go orienteering

Maps are intriguing: an exciting mixture of pictorial clues and secret code, to be cracked only by those who can navigate. Learning to read a map and use a compass is enjoyable and incredibly useful too, even in an age of digital navigation. Unravelling the clues that lie in the landscape and applying them to the map (and vice versa) is fun and rewarding in a way that following a dot on a screen just isn't. It's also important that, should your device's batteries run out or you drop it off a cliff, you can revert to your trusty map and still be able to find your way.

Orienteering is an exciting and challenging outdoor sport that's a great workout for both mind and body. The aim is to navigate between control points marked on an orienteering map, either as a fun activity that makes a great day out for families of any age or as a competitive sport where the aim is to complete the course in the fastest time, picking your own route between controls.

Orienteering can be done on foot, on a bike – or even on skis. There are permanent orienteering courses all over the country – you may have seen the posts with an orange and white marker – with distances ranging from little over a mile (1.6km) to over 10 miles (16km). They're everywhere from city centres and urban parks to woodland, mountain and moorland. British Orienteering (www.britishorienteering.org.uk) have a

TOP TIPS

- The quickest way between control points isn't always a straight line – look for good paths and routes that have the least change in height.
- Most National Trust places that offer orienteering have downloadable maps on their websites, or pop in to the visitor centre onsite for a map.

Learning to use a compass at Brancaster, Norfolk.

GREAT FOR

LEARNING • NATURE • ACTIVE

FUN FACTS

- Orienteering is a recognised sport that you can compete in to a high level. There's a British, European and world championships held each year.

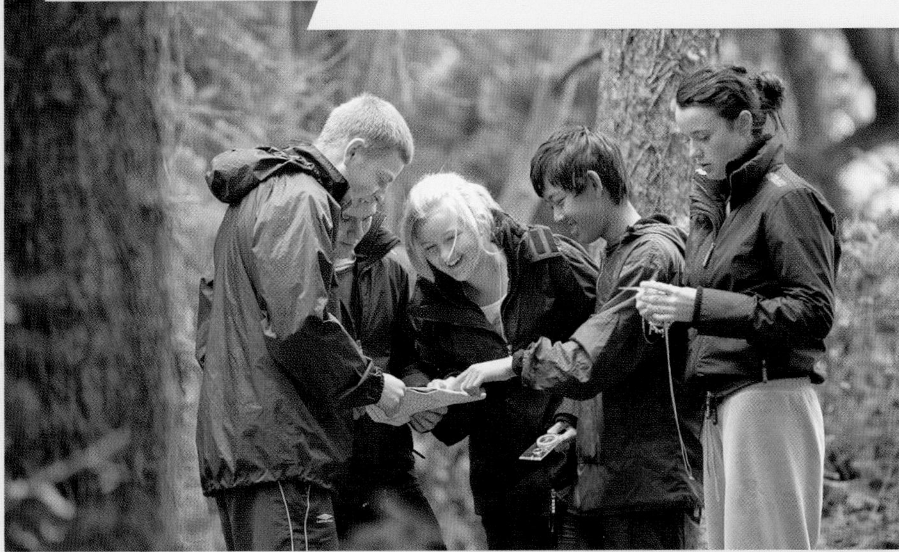

Planning the next checkpoint at Castle Ward, Northern Island.

database of all permanent courses, and you can search for your nearest using your postcode.

Many National Trust places have fixed orienteering courses that are a great way to explore the area while improving your navigation skills at the same time. Maps are available with the controls marked on them – all you have to do is find them and write down the unique code. Coed Berthlwyd in southern Snowdonia is a fantastic place to go orienteering, with five different courses graded from easy for beginners to hard. Finding your way through this wild and beautiful landscape, keeping an eye out for each marker as you go, is a thrilling experience. Bear in mind that the hard courses may take you into remote locations so you'll need to be proficient at navigation before you try them. Snowdonia is a real hub for outdoor adventure and there's so much for families to do, from walking and rock climbing in the spectacular mountains to swimming and kayaking in the lakes (llŷns in Welsh).

HEAD

45

Go orienteering

Where to go

SOUTH WEST

Stonebarrow permanent orienteering course

Golden Cap Estate, Morcombelake, Bridport, Dorset DT6 6RA

 (not National Trust) 

Walk or run around the glorious Golden Cap estate with views out across the Channel on one of three permanent orienteering courses. The Short Course is 0.6 miles (1km) with 7 control markers, the Medium Course is 1.2 miles (2km) with 10 control markers and the Long Course is 2 miles (3.2km) with 13 control markers. Each red-and-white marker is affixed to a wooden structure and has a two-letter code for you to collect. The courses start and finish at the National Trust shop.

SOUTH WEST

Sherborne Park Estate

Lodge Park, Aldsworth, near Cheltenham, Gloucestershire GL54 3PP

Sherborne is a working estate with great, family-friendly walks, three of which are well-waymarked. Make sure you visit the eighteenth-century water meadows where, if you're lucky, you might spot otters, water voles and dragonflies. The permanent orienteering trail here is a perfect introduction to the sport, with 13 markers set over a 1-mile (1.6km) course.

WEST MIDLANDS

Attingham Park

Atcham, Shrewsbury, Shropshire SY4 4TP

Explore the woods, discover the natural playfield and have a go at orienteering in the grounds of this eighteenth-century mansion with a turbulent past. It's also a great place to explore the river in an open canoe or go tree climbing. Produce from the walled garden is available in the shop.

Orienteering lesson at Brancaster, Norfolk.

46 Sleep in a bothy

There's been an explosion of interest in camping recently, with campsites opening across the country offering everything from five-star luxury, complete with hot tubs, to a meadow with a tap in it. Going camping is a great way to have a low-cost, adventurous holiday with a family of any age: the kids love getting back to nature, sleeping out in the open with the owls to lull them to sleep, cooking over an open fire and having adventures in the great outdoors every day. But sleeping under canvas isn't for everyone and bothies provide an excellent alternative, being placed in remote and beautiful places with a real feeling of getting away from it all, whilst still having four solid walls and a roof over your head. They're also perfect if you're heading off without the car for a weekend and don't fancy carrying a tent, but much more of an adventure than a B&B, and many accept dogs too.

We stayed in the National Trust's Peppercombe Bothy for a few nights in the summer. The tiny white building sits perched above the glittering sea in a peaceful valley on Devon's north coast and is reached up a bumpy track that's an adventure in its own right. It's a former pigsty, which doesn't sound too glamorous, but it has everything you need for a wild, no-frills family adventure. The surroundings are glorious: a tangle of lush greenery, winding woodland paths, a little private garden with a picnic bench – and it's just a few minutes' walk from a secluded pebble beach where we spent a

FUN FACTS

- Bothies were traditionally used to house farm workers or as refuges in remote or mountainous places.
- Bothies are back-to-basics accommodation, often with no electricity and few facilities.
- The National Trust has five bothies, each in its own spectacular location.

Reading in the top bunk of the bothy.

Sunset over Peppercombe Bothy, Devon.

happy day paddling and skimming stones without seeing a single other person. It's basic but there's running water, sink and loo (in a shed out the back), and it has has breathtaking views out over the Bristol Channel to the island of Lundy.

We were fortunate enough to witness a spectacular sunset while we were there, and we sat in contentment watching the sky blaze with pink, red and gold – who needs TV anyway?

There are five National Trust bothies spread across the country, from Sussex to the Lake District. Peppercombe is one of the more basic, with some having access to showers and other facilities.

TOP TIPS

- Bothies make great bases or stopovers for exploring – feeling wild and remote without the need to carry a tent.
- There's no bedding provided and beds are usually fairly hard platforms, so take camping mats and sleeping bags to ensure a warm and comfortable night.
- There's likely to be no mobile reception or internet nearby; make the most of it and bring a book instead!

GREAT FOR

CHALLENGES • NATURE • ACTIVE • DOG-FRIENDLY

46

Sleep in a bothy

Where to go

SOUTH WEST

Foreland Bothy, Devon

Countisbury, Lynton, Devon EX35 6NE

Foreland Bothy is a simple building with sleeping platforms located in a spectacular location on the South West Coast Path. There's open moorland, woodland and coast to explore nearby – and the pretty villages of Lynton and Lynmouth not far away.

SOUTH EAST

Gumber Bothy, Sussex

Gumber Farm, Arundel BN18 0RN

With no vehicular access and a 2-mile (3.2km) walk from the nearest car park, staying at Gumber Bothy is a real adventure. The bothy and adjoining campsite are simple but well equipped. The estate is great for exploring and wildlife spotting (there's a badger set close to the bothy).

NORTH WEST

Holme Wood Bothy, Cumbria

Loweswater, Cumbria CA13 0RU

Remote and secluded, Holme Wood Bothy offers basic accommodation in a truly breathtaking location just a few metres away from the shore of Loweswater, with just the owls and woodland creatures to keep you company. It's a great base for some really wild adventures.

Sunset over the sea, viewed from Peppercombe Bothy, Devon.

SOUTH WEST

Peppercombe Bothy, Devon

Bideford, Devon EX39 5QD

Nestled in a secluded, wooded valley with views out across the sea and a nearby pebble beach, Peppercombe makes a great base for exploring the dramatic North Devon coast.

NORTH WEST

Watendlath Bothy, Cumbria

Borrowdale, Cumbria CA12 5UW

Sitting on the shores of the tarn of the same name, high in a picturesque Lake District valley, Watendlath is a perfect choice for a wild family adventure. Accommodation is basic but does include a shower, hob, fridge, bunks and wood-burning stove.

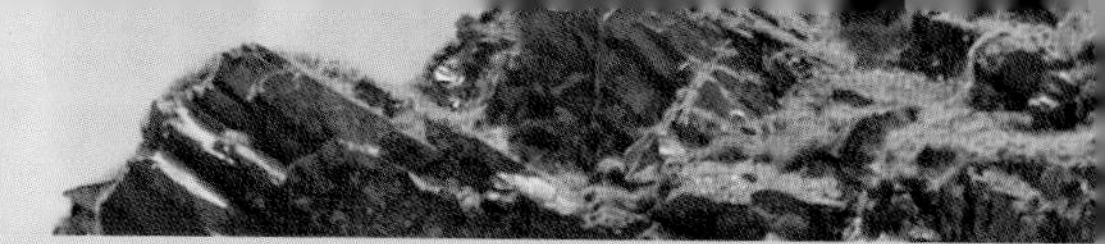

GIANT LEAPS: EXTREME CHALLENGES FOR THE BRAVE AND BOLD

These extreme adventures aren't for the faint-hearted, but master the skills to do them safely and they'll provide you with a lifetime of exhilaration and enjoyment. They're perfect entertainment for older kids, teenagers and grown-ups too. Learn the ropes in climbing and abseiling; ride the waves on a surfboard; discover hidden coves in a sea kayak or scramble up a waterfall – once you start adventuring, you'll never want to stop.

47 Go ghyll scrambling and coasteering

The Lake District is an absolutely brilliant place to head to if you're a family that loves adventuring in the great outdoors. It's impossible not to be inspired and excited by the dramatic landscapes here: vast rippling lakes, towering, rugged mountains and inviting trails that loop through grassy river valleys and craggy rock faces. It's why we love the Lakes and head back there whenever we can. One of our favourite discoveries for a fun-for-all family excursion is ghyll scrambling. This adventurous sport simply involves ascending or descending a gorge that has been cut by falling water through the underlying rock. The best ghylls for scrambling have jumps and slides into deep plunge pools, swirling sections of white water, short sections of swimming and some scrambling up and down rocky sections. It's a great year-round activity that can be made easy for younger children or those not wanting to take the plunge, or extreme for anyone looking for a really exciting adventure. In general, the more water there is in a ghyll the more exciting it will be to scramble, so during winter and after heavy rainfall is the time for the most adventurous only.

Supervised ghyll scrambling in Stickle Ghyll, Cumbria.

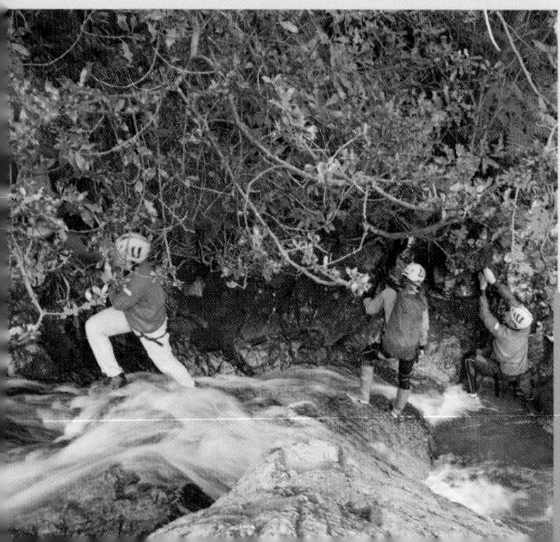

Although there's nothing stopping you from exploring a ghyll on your own, a safe and enjoyable way to go about it is to join one of the many groups that head out from outdoor activity centres all over the Lakes. Having fun is essential, but so is staying safe, so you'll be kitted out with a helmet, wetsuit, buoyancy aid, jacket and even neoprene socks in colder weather. All specialist equipment is provided and your instructors will be qualified and

GREAT FOR

WATER • EXTREME • ACTIVE

experienced with a good knowledge of the local area and conditions. Depending on the company you go with and the location of the ghyll you should usually expect to be out for between two and four hours. You don't need to be a strong swimmer to go ghyll scrambling as you'll be wearing buoyant kit and there's always a helpful instructor or two on hand to help you out. Most kids will love ghyll scrambling and it's easily adapted to suit all levels of bravery and ability, but most companies specify a minimum age of 7.

Coasteering at Mullion Cove, Cornwall.

TOP TIPS

- Ghyll scrambling can be tailored to suit all abilities and if you book with an outdoor activity centre all safety equipment is provided, so don't be afraid to give it a go!
- Take plenty of warm, dry clothing to change into once you've finished scrambling.
- 'Ghyll' is a northern English term for a gorge or mountain stream. If you're looking for a similar activity in the rest of the UK it might be called 'gorge scrambling', 'canyoning' or, if it's on sea cliffs, 'coasteering'.

Where to go

NORTH WEST

Stickle Ghyll, Great Langdale, Cumbria

A great, year-round ghyll where all tricky sections are easily avoidable. Lovely, family-friendly National Trust-run pub at the finish.

Esk Ghyll, Eskdale, Cumbria

(not National Trust)
Fantastic scrambling in a remote location that's better for older children. About an hour's walk-in from the foot of the Hardknott Pass.

Stoneycroft Ghyll, near Keswick, Cumbria

(not National Trust)
Just a five-minute drive from Keswick, Stoneycroft is considered by many to be one of the best ghylls for scrambling. It's a particularly enjoyable descent, with lots of steep slides into deep pools and fantastic views. There's a canyoning option for those looking for a more extreme option, with abseils and waterfalls to tackle.

NATIONWIDE

There are excellent ghyll/gorge scrambling locations around the country, in particular around Hathersage and Matlock in Derbyshire, and Exmoor and Dartmoor in Somerset and Devon. Coasteering can also be found in many coastal locations.

Preparing to jump in at Mullion Cove, Cornwall.

48 A sea kayaking adventure

Nothing beats exploring the coast in a sea kayak: the gentle rise-and-fall of the sea, craggy cliffs that reach into the sky, sun, wind and salt spray on your skin, the evocative call of seabirds and the freedom to paddle around sea stacks, delve into secret caves and coves and land on hidden beaches. It's a wonderful change of perspective, and a fantastic family adventure.

Sea kayaks are longer and narrower than multi-purpose or freestyle designs, but much more stable than marathon kayaks and relatively easy to steer in a straight line. They seat one or two people and are designed for paddling longer distances in a wide range of weather conditions. They may also have covered sections for stowing equipment – great for longer expeditions or family adventures. Many hire centres also use sit-on-top kayaks that are very stable and safer for beginners. Sea kayaking is most suited to older children and being confident in

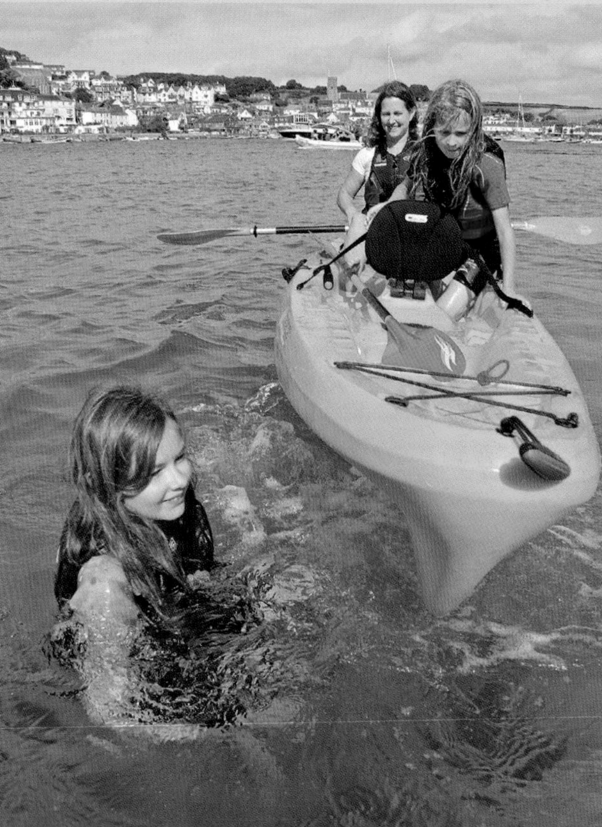

TOP TIPS

- If you haven't kayaked before – especially on the sea – it's a good idea to attend a beginners' course, such as the BCU 1 star award, before heading off on your own.
- Paddling efficiently and in a straight line takes a bit of practice! Stick with it and you'll improve quickly.

water is essential as it's quite common to end up doing a bit of swimming. For enjoyable, safe kayaking you'll also need a helmet and a buoyancy aid.

If you haven't done much kayaking before, or you're heading out in an area you're unfamiliar with, it's a great idea to book onto a course or guided paddle. There are many excellent places to kayak all around Britain's coast, with plenty of choice when it comes to hiring boats too. Cornwall's warm climate and stunning coastline makes it a perfect place to try out kayaking. Lizard Adventure, (lizardadventure.co.uk) in south Cornwall, runs guided sea kayaking trips around the beautiful blue-green seas off the Lizard Peninsula. You'll be led by an experienced guide, provided with all the kit you'll need and taught the basics you need to explore safely, as well as having a hugely enjoyable day.

The National Trust Sea Kayaking Festival is held each May in Stackpole, Pembrokeshire. This fantastic weekend offers two full days of guided exploration around this stunning area, with each trip graded for difficulty and led by experienced guides. There's plenty of fun for all, with talks, food, camping and live music. See page 62 for more details.

Kayaking at Old Harry's Rocks, Dorset.

GREAT FOR WATER • NATURE • ACTIVE

48

A sea kayaking adventure

Where to go

There are lots of National Trust places that are perfect for a sea kayaking adventure. Many have boat and equipment hire too, so all you need to do is turn up ready to get exploring! Here are some top places to try:

1. **Stackpole, Pembrokeshire**
2. **Fowey, Cornwall**
3. **Salcombe, Devon**
4. **Studland Bay, Dorset**
5. **The Lizard, Cornwall**
6. **Boggle Hole, North Yorkshire**

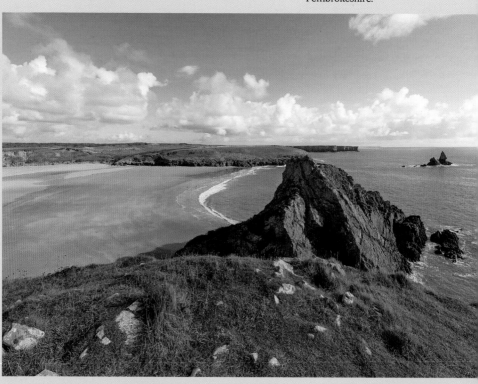

Broadhaven Beach near Stackpole, Pembrokeshire.

Boggle Hole
Stackpole
Studland Bay
Fowey
Salcombe
Lizard

49 Rock climbing and abseiling

Rock climbing is a great activity for kids of all ages: learning to move over tricky terrain, using ropes and tying knots and working together as a team are invaluable skills – and the places climbing takes you can't be beaten. There's a fairly gradual progression in climbing, from indoor walls up through top roping (climbing with a rope above you) to lead climbing (placing protective 'gear' as you go and clipping the rope in for safety) and even soloing (no ropes at all!) for the extremely brave or slightly crazy... Children can start climbing on a top rope as soon as they're keen to do so and often find it a much more natural activity than adults. Having the skills to go climbing together safely opens up a whole new world of adventure, but if you're not quite ready to do it all yourself or want to learn the skills for the future there are plenty of excellent, highly qualified instructors ready to teach you the ropes. Outdoor climbing

GREAT FOR

EXTREME • NATURE • ACTIVE

instructors need to have a minimum of an SPA qualification, and preferably they will have an MIA or MIC qualification too.

Many indoor walls have family sessions or groups specifically for younger children; these are a great way to learn climbing skills and are fun, sociable and often held weekly. Once you have progressed outdoors, some of the best beginner-friendly climbs are on 'slabs': easy-angled rock faces with plenty of good hand and foot holds on them. An instructor will teach you all the basic skills you need to start top roping, including how to check harnesses are fastened correctly, how to tie in to a rope, how to set up anchors and belays, and simple techniques for climbing.

Left: Climbing in the Ogwen Valley, Gwynedd.

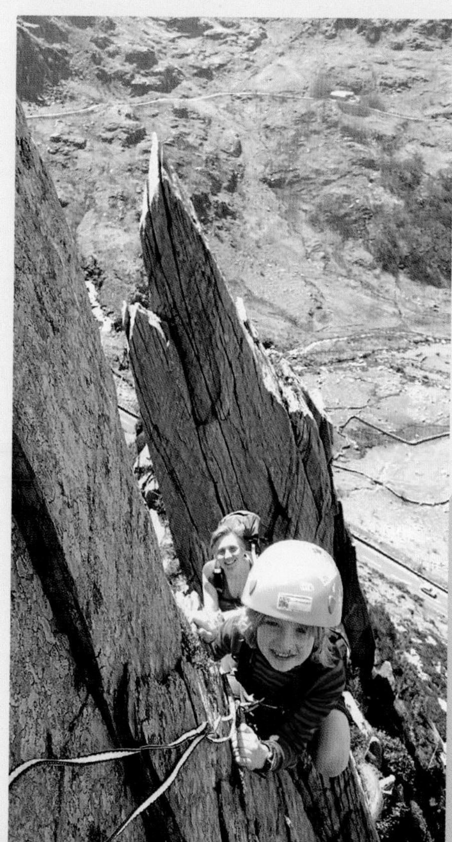

If you enjoy climbing and are keen to do more there are plenty of safe, easy rock climbs all over the country and all you need are climbing shoes, helmets, harnesses, a rope and some equipment for anchoring to the rock. It's essential all of these items are new: you'll be entrusting your safety entirely to them. Speak to the staff in your local climbing shop to find out more.

For many climbers, abseiling is simply a method of getting back down again, but it can be undertaken as a fun activity in its own right. You can abseil off bridges, down rocks and out of trees, and it's a good way to descend into hard-to-access places to explore. Abseiling is also, however, more dangerous than climbing itself, so stick with abseils organised by experts and don't attempt to set one up yourself until you're absolutely sure what you're doing.

Left: Multi-pitch climbing in North Wales.

TOP TIPS

- If you're just starting out climbing it's a good idea to have a few sessions at an indoor wall. Here you'll learn basic skills that will feel more familiar when you're outside.

Where to go

WALES

Idwal Slabs, Ogwen, Carneddau, Snowdonia

Snowdonia's Carneddau range is a place of rugged mountains, soaring ridgelines, crystal-clear lakes and dramatic views. It's a wonderful place to explore, with almost endless possibilities for adventure. The rocky slabs at Idwal are great for beginners and local outdoor centres including Plas y Brenin (not National Trust) in Capel Curig run courses to show you the basics.

NORTH WEST

Brimham Rocks

Summerbridge, Harrogate, North Yorkshire HG3 4DW

Brimham's varied, rocky landscape makes it a popular venue with climbers – and a great place to start. The National Trust works in partnership with Harrogate Climbing Centre to provide rock climbing courses for all ages and abilities.

NORTHERN IRELAND

Mourne Mountains, County Down

The National Trust works in partnership with Clearsky Adventure to provide rock climbing courses for all in the spectacular Mourne Mountains. Why not stay in one of the Trust's holiday cottages or camp nearby (not National Trust)? There's so much to explore here, from the rugged peaks all the way down to the sea.

Climbing at Brimham Rocks, Nidderdale, North Yorkshire.

50 Surf's up!

The National Trust looks after some 775 miles (1,250km) of the UK's beautiful coastline. It's not surprising, therefore, that among these glorious stretches lie some of the country's best surf beaches. Surfing and bodyboarding are great fun for family adventures: what could be better than spending the day on a beautiful beach, taking in the sights, the sounds and the wildlife, learning new skills, playing in the waves and even cooking up a feast on a beach barbecue at the end of the day?

Surfing requires a lot of practice and usually some tuition to take on the waves with confidence. Mastering 'popping up' on your board takes most people at least five sessions. But once you have the hang of it it's an incredibly addictive sport with a great social side too. If you're not bothered about standing up on your board then bodyboarding is much easier to master, and even as a complete beginner you can have a lot of fun playing in the shallow whitewater and letting the waves bring you in.

Running down to the surf at Portstewart Strand, County Londonderry.

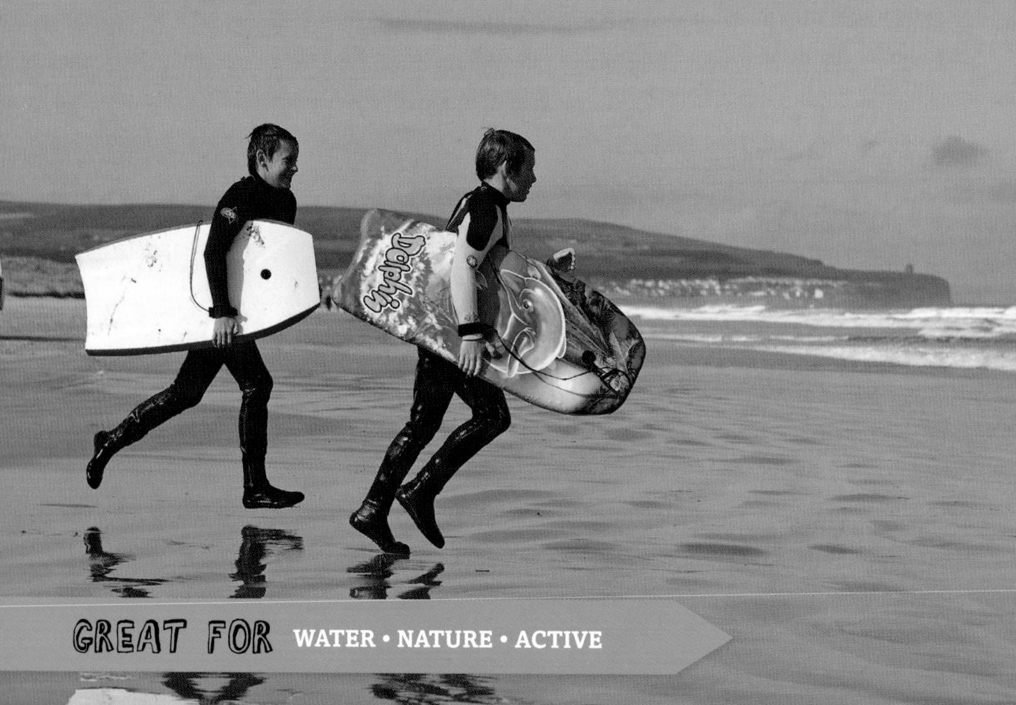

GREAT FOR WATER • NATURE • ACTIVE

The Llŷn Peninsula, Gwynedd, is one of our favourite places for surfing. It has everything: fine crescents of golden sand; surf that's perfect for beginners and experts alike; remote spots where you can watch wildlife and have the beach to yourself; or bustling family-filled holiday hotspots. The wonderfully-named Hell's Mouth is a perfect 4-mile (6.5km) stretch of sand where the surf is consistently good due to swell coming in from the Atlantic. The best area for beginners is usually the middle of the bay, whereas the reef at the northern end produces the best surf for the more experienced.

The sea is at its warmest in late summer and early autumn, although the seas around the UK could never exactly be described as 'warm'. A wetsuit will make your surfing or bodyboarding experience much more pleasant, insulating you from the water and adding a little buoyancy and protection too.

SAFETY NOTE: please be vigilant and never let kids go in the sea alone. Big swell days are not suitable for beginners.

Above: Riding a wave on a bodyboard.

TOP TIPS

- Beginner boards and wetsuits are available for hire at many locations.
- Some beaches have lifeguards present for extra safety – essential if you're just learning to surf.
- The weather and tide have a big effect on sea conditions: learn to read forecasts and tide tables and if in doubt seek expert advice.
- Check surf forecasts online at: magicseaweed.com

Where to go

Playing in the surf at Portstewart Strand.

SOUTH EAST

Compton Bay, Isle of Wight

With the best surf on the Isle of Wight, Compton Bay is a relatively-quiet, family-friendly beach with easy access from the car park (free for NT members). There's plenty to suit all abilities and great swimming and paddling too. Dogs welcome in most areas.

NORTHERN IRELAND

Portstewart Strand, County Down

A great beach for watersports, there's a designated jet-ski area, keeping them away from swimmers and surfers, and lifeguard cover in July and August. There are refreshments and a shop at the Visitor Centre and parking on the beach.

WALES

Rhossili, Gower Peninsula, Swansea

Voted one of Britain's best beaches, Rhossili's 3-mile (5km) crescent of golden sand and generally calm seas make it an enjoyable surfing destination. There's a shop and café (not National Trust) in the village adjacent to the beach.

Freshwater West, Pembrokeshire

Known locally as Freshwest this is considered one of the most consistent surf spots in Wales. Caution: Not for beginners or swimmers due to strong rip currents.

Porthor, Llŷn Peninsula

Also known as Whistling Sands because of the noise made by the sand particles as they rub together, Porthor is a beautiful, peaceful beach that's great for surfing and bodyboarding.

SOUTH WEST

Sandymouth Bay, Cornwall

A beautiful beach close to a National Trust car park. Take care not to get cut off at high tide.

Rhossili Beach, Swansea.

Places and activities index

abseiling 214–17
adventure journals 114–15
Apple Day 61
archaeology 138–41

barefoot walking 68–70, 71, 77
bat walks 146–9
beaches
 Big Beach Clean 145
 winter adventure 56–9
Bedfordshire
 Dunstable Downs and Whipsnade Estate 126
 Dunstable Kite Festival 128, 130, 131
bee houses 112
boat trips 64–7
bothies 200–3
bouldering 172–4, 175
Buckinghamshire
 Cliveden 65
 Hughenden Manor 27
 Stowe 72, 73, 75
bug hotels 112–13
bushcraft 168–71

Cambridgeshire
 Waterclose Meadows 152
 Wicken Fen 162, 179
 Wimpole Estate 98, 101, 107
camping 62, 88–91, 150–2, 153, 176–9
canoeing and kayaking 180–3, 210–12, 213
castle exploration 94–7
cave exploration 108–11
Cheshire
 Dunham Massey 116
 Lyme 107, 131
climbing
 bouldering 172–4, 175
 mountains 164–7
 rock climbing 214–17
 towers 136–7
 trees 116–19
coasteering 206–8, 209
Cornwall
 Antony House 123
 Cotehele 105
 Fowey 212
 Godolphin 70
 Gribbin Head 136, 137
 Highertown Campsite 30, 33, 152
 Holywell and Crantock 58
 Lanhydrock 107, 185, 187
 The Lizard 211
 Lizard Point 83
 Mullion Cove 209
 Penrose 107
 Sandymouth Bay 221
 St Anthony Head 108, 160
 Teneriffe Farm 152
 Trelissick 117
County Antrim
 Carrick-a-Rede 158, 158
 Giant's Causeway 54, 185
County Armargh, Ardress House 98
County Down
 Castle Ward Campsite 91, 152
 Mount Stewart 38
 Mourne Mountains 217
 Murlough National Nature Reserve 161, 162
 Portstewart Strand 218, 220
 Strangford Lough 24, 181, 194
County Fermanagh
 Castle Coole 107
 Crom 152, 182
 Florence Court 52
County Londonderry
 Downhill Demesne 62, 131
 Portstewart Strand 59
Cumbria
 Aira Force 189, 190
 Allan Bank 19
 Cathedral Quarries 108, 110
 Coniston Water 185
 Derwentwater 75, 156, 158, 182
 Eskdale 18, 104, 133, 208
 Fell Foot 107, 117
 Footprint 169, 170
 fossil hunting 54
 Great Langdale 89, 151, 152, 174
 Hill Top, Sawrey 84–5, 86
 Hoathwaite 152
 Holme Wood bothy 202
 Keswick Mountain Festival 62
 Lake Coniston 87
 Lake Windermere 85, 87
 Low Wray 88, 89, 91, 152, 171, 180–1
 St Bees 174
 Stickle Ghyll 76, 166, 206, 208
 Stoneycroft Ghyll 208
 Tarn Hows 72, 79, 85
 Wasdale 152, 194
 Watendlath bothy 203
 Wray Castle 84, 85, 95, 97
cycling 184–7

den building 12, 77
Derbyshire
 Burbage South 174
 Edale Valley 184–5
 Kedleston Hall 170
 Longshaw Estate 119, 134, 135
 Mam Tor 124, 127, 165, 167
 Manifold Way 185
Devon
 Arlington Court 52, 145
 Buckland Abbey 63
 Castle Drogo 94
 Dartmoor 178
 Foreland bothy 202
 Greenway 65, 66
 Hembury and Holne Woods 28
 Hound Tor 174
 Killerton 40, 44, 62, 107
 Lundy Island 157, 158
 Lydford Gorge 188–9, 190
 Parke Estate 18, 20, 60
 Parke Estate, Dartmoor 107
 Peppercombe bothy 200–1, 203
 Plymbridge Woods 107, 135
 Prattshayes 152
 Salcombe 181, 212
 Saltram 149
 Watersmeet 183
 Wembury 22, 25
Dorset
 Brownsea Island 65, 156–7, 158
 Corfe Castle 81, 94, 95, 96
 Golden Cap Estate 152, 199
 Hardy Monument 137
 Jurassic Coast 52, 53, 54
 Old Harry's Rocks 211
 Studland and Knoll Beach 28, 194, 212

East Yorkshire, fossil hunting 54
Essex
 Hatfield Forest 44, 46, 107
 Northey Island 62, 158

farm help 98–101
festivals 60–2, 63, 131, 211
film sets 120–3
foraging 26–9

fossil hunting 52–4, 55

ghyll scrambling 15, 206–8
glamping 88–91
Gloucestershire
Chedworth Roman Villa 140
Dyrham Park 148
Sherborne Park Estate 199
Woodchester Park 118

Hampshire, Bramshaw Commons 187
hedgehog house 113
Herefordshire
Berrington Hall 131
Croft Castle 20
Hertfordshire, Ashridge Estate 123, 185, 186

ice skating 77
island adventure 156–8, 159
Isle of Wight
Bembridge Windmill 137
Compton Bay 194, 220
fossil hunting 54
St Helens Duver 24
Ventnor Downs 83

journal making 114–15

kayaking 62, 210–12, 213
Kent
Emmetts Garden 38
Knole 137
South Foreland Lighthouse 130, 137
St Margaret's Bay 81
White Cliffs of Dover 83
kite flying 62, 77, 128–31

lake circumnavigation 72–5
Lincolnshire, Belton House 107, 118
literary adventures 84–7

Merseyside
Formby beach 54, 56
Speke Hall 119
Middlesex, Osterley Park 107
mountain biking 184–7
mountain climbing 164–7
mud ktichins 77

night walking 30–3
Norfolk
Blakeney Point 54, 64, 66
Blickling Estate 80, 107
Brancaster 104
Sheringham Park 33, 107, 168
North Yorkshire
Boggle Hole 212
Brimham Rocks 217
Fountains Abbey and Studley Royal 51, 107
Malham Tarn Estate 146, 148
Roseberry Topping 29
Northumberland
Cragside 68, 70, 71, 72–3
Druridge Bay 83
Farne Islands 64–5
Hadrian's Wall and Housesteads Fort 139, 141
Lindisfarne 64, 94, 158
Wallington 21, 47
Nottinghamshire, Clumber Park 5, 89, 90, 107, 152

orienteering 196–9
Oxfordshire, White Horse Hill 144

Parkruns 106–7
pond dipping 5, 47

rafting 102–5
rock climbing 214–17
rock pooling 22–5

sea kayaking 210–12, 213
Shropshire
Attingham Park 39, 199
Carding Mill Valley 83, 194
Dudmaston 50
Long Mynd 32
sledging 124–7
Somerset
Bath Skyline 107
Brean Down 143
Leigh Woods 184, 186
Montacute House 107
Wellington Monument 78
South Downs 54
Staffordshire
Downs Bank 126
Holy Austin Rock Houses 111
stream walking 132–5
Suffolk
Dunwich beach 70, 83
Lavingham Guildhall 120, 121, 122
Sutton Hoo 138, 139, 140
sunrise watching 80–3
surfing 218–21
Surrey
Belvedere Tower 137
Box Hill 78, 79, 125
Dapdune Wharf Navigations Office 66
Leith Hill Tower 136, 137
Polesden Lacey 152
River Wey 65
Sussex
Bateman's 85, 87
Birling Gap and the Seven Sisters 23, 54, 68
Bodiam Castle 94, 95, 96, 137
Gumber bothy 202
Saddlescombe Estate 152
Slindon Estate 152
swimming 73, 77, 192–4

time travel 138–41
tower climbing 136–7
tree climbing 116–19
Tyne & Wear
Gibside 101, 107, 171
The Leas 107
Souter Lighthouse 137

volunteering 142–5

Wales
Abereiddi 54
Bodnant Garden 105
Brecon Beacons 83, 126, 165, 166, 177
Chirk Castle 137
Colby Woodland Garden 34, 107, 134
Dolaucothi Estate 45, 152
Freshwater West 221
Henrhyd 189, 191
Llanerchaeron 98, 101
Ll n Peninsula 219, 221
Lydstep Caverns 109, 110
Ogwen Valley 217
Penbryn beach, Cardigan Bay 31
Penrhyn Castle 107, 162
RAC boulders 174
Rhossili 58, 221
Stackpole Estate 50, 62, 149, 211, 212
Tredegar House 107
wassailing 60
waterfalls 188–91
waymarked trail following 18–21
West Yorkshire
Marsden Moor 83
Nostell Priory 107
wild weather adventures 76–9
wilderness survival 168–71
wildlife safari
lakes and ponds 46–51
parks and gardens 34–9
woodland and forest 40–5
wildlife tracking 160–2
Wiltshire
Avebury 81, 82–3, 138–9, 140
Great Chalfield Manor 35, 47
Lacock Abbey and village 120–1, 122
Stourhead 73, 74, 108–9, 137
wind chimes 77
Worcestershire, Croome 137

Picture Credits

Acknowledgements

Our heartfelt thanks to the following people: Katie Bond, Lucy Smith, Peter Taylor, the brilliant employees and volunteers at the National Trust, in particular Beth at Dyrham Park, Amy Feldman and Rob Joules, the Benson, Perkins, Foggan and Triner families, Ros, Tony and Amy, Ian, Dawn, Grace, Evie and Olive Everett-Kelway, Matt Heason & family, SoulPad, Neil Cox & family, the Pryer Family, Robert Tilt, Joe & Zana, Long Valley Yurts, woodmatters.org.uk, Andy Cavanagh & family, Dan, Tan & Rose, the Wainwright family, and, finally, to E & H for sharing with us the greatest adventure of all.